IT HAPPENED IN SCHOOL

NOTE: This book is based on the life experiences of a teacher and coach. Some of the content was developed from stories told to the author by colleagues and used with their permission. In every story, effort was given to ensure accuracy.

Published by Emerald Book Company
Austin, TX
www.emeraldbookcompany.com

Distributed by Emerald Book Company

For ordering information or special discounts for bulk purchases, please contact Emerald Book Company at PO Box 91869, Austin, TX 78709, 512.891.6100.

Publisher's Cataloging-In-Publication Data
(Prepared by The Donohue Group, Inc.)
Crosby, Robert Hughey, 1948-
  It happened in school / Bob Crosby. -- 1st ed.
    p. ; cm.

4138O311   9/09
ISBN: 978-1-934572-15-3

1. Crosby, Robert Hughey, 1948- --Career in teaching. 2. Teachers--Anecdotes. 3. Teaching--Anecdotes. I. Title.

LA23 .C76 2009
371.1/002/07   2009920750

Part of the Tree Neutral™ program, which offsets the number of trees consumed in the production and printing of this book by taking proactive steps, such as planting trees in direct proportion to the number of trees used: www.treeneutral.com

Printed in the United States of America on acid-free paper

09 10 11 12 13 14   10 9 8 7 6 5 4 3 2 1

First Edition

IT HAPPENED IN SCHOOL

50 STORIES OF ACTUAL
CLASSROOM/ATHLETIC FIELD
HAPPENINGS BOUND TO PUT
A SMILE ON YOUR FACE

BOB CROSBY

EMERALD
BOOK CO.

This book is dedicated to all those students and athletes who helped make my teaching career so much fun. In addition, I dedicate it to my family and to my faculty mates with whom I have shared so many stories and so many good times. Last but not least, I dedicate it to The Snooper, truly man's best friend!

Special thanks to my wife Mikki and to Bill Tobias and Randa Flinn for their support and proofreading skills.

CON

ENTS

F🍎REWORD

Northeast High School is a fairly typical school. We have some smart kids; we have some dumb kids. We have some annoying kids; we have some kids that any parent would be proud to claim. We also have an excellent faculty and administration. Okay, there may be some among us who aren't really excellent, but, no, I will not name them in these pages.

This book is all about fun. Some of the stories included herein happened to my faculty mates rather than to me, and it is with their permission that I have recounted them here. One or two of the incidents happened at my son and daughter's school, Fort Lauderdale High, and even though in some cases I was not there to see them personally, they still qualify for the book because they did, in fact, "happen in school."

It has been my distinct pleasure (well, sometimes at least) to teach at NHS for the past 33 years. (It has never ceased to amaze me that students and faculty alike have often referred to our school as NEHS. How can that be correct when North-east is all one word?) Anyway, I teach English and journalism but have coached over 35 seasons of athletics as well. Included among the teams I have coached are softball, volleyball, base-ball, football, and even golf teams. In addition, as the jour-nalism teacher/adviser, I have overseen the publication of 27 yearbooks and 24 school newspapers. *The Sun-Sentinel,* our local newspaper, even named me softball Coach of the Year in 1982 and journalism Adviser of the Year in 2007. With that much contact with kids in so many different areas of school and over such a wide range of years, there have been numer-ous incidents of all kinds that have indelibly ingrained them-selves in my brain. However, the funny ones are the ones I have chosen to recount here.

This year is my 35th and final year of teaching. Before mov-ing on to the much-anticipated world of retirement, I wanted to set down in print for the universe to see just what fun for me teaching has been over the years.

Fun? Yes, fun. Sure there are fights and drugs and profanity and student apathy and many other negative things in schools, but who wants to read about that stuff? Well, everybody does I guess.

As one of my colleagues said when I told her I was going to leave out all that negative stuff, "You won't have to worry about your book being a best seller."

Nevertheless, this book only highlights fun things that have happened in school. Someone else can write *The Wicked, Depressing, Sad, Traumatic Things that Happened in School.* But for those readers out there who can't do without the sug-gestive, the bawdy, the foul language, or the occasional in-nuendo in their reading, there are a few chapters herein that may be rated "PG-13" rather just plain old "G" like the rest of them. Those chapters have asterisks in their chapter titles and are duly noted by way of footnotes at the bottom of the first pages of their chapters; readers should read those chapters with the understanding that sometimes in school language and situations are not always lily white. In other words, don't haul off and read those to your eight-year-old unless you are prepared to answer a few questions along the way.

It might have been wiser to wait until I retire to write this book, but being a Florida State University alumnus I have heard the 'Noles head man Bobby Bowden say many times in response to the question of when he will retire, "I'm not in any hurry to retire because once you retire, there's just one big event left."

That comment has had a distinct impact on me especially since there have been some teacher friends of mine who have retired after long teaching careers only to die within a year or so after turning in their dry erase markers. In some cases I had the feeling they just didn't know how to handle their leisure time. I don't expect that to happen to me. After all, I have proven summer after summer for the past 34 years that I can handle leisure time with the best of them. But one never knows what's going to happen, so I have gone ahead with the writing of the book.

I hope you enjoy my recollections of 35 years of teaching high school as much as I have enjoyed reliving them once again.

"WORLD'S GREATEST COACH"

I had been coaching girls' volleyball at our school for about six years, and we were about to embark on what promised to be a pretty good season considering we had most of our team back from the previous year. I was excited about it and so were the girls.

After practice the day before the first game, I finished my pep talk and sent them home . . . but they didn't go.

"Coach, we have something we want to give you," the captain said with all the other girls clustered around us.

"Oh, really, what?" I asked suspiciously.

"We bought you a little good luck charm. It's . . . uh . . . a key chain."

It was wrapped in a small box. I opened it, and sure enough it was a key chain. But this wasn't an ordinary key chain . . . this one had a very touching message on it. It had a bright yellow background with a silver whistle pictured on it. Beneath the whistle were inscribed the words "World's Greatest Coach."

"Wow, thanks, you guys. That's very nice, but we'll see how 'great' I am tomorrow. You know how great a coach is perceived to be is totally determined by how well his team plays," I said trying to take advantage of any little motivational opportunity that came my way.

They totally ignored my motivational ploy. They were much more concerned with the gift itself.

"Are you going to put all of your keys on it?" one of the girls asked.

Still trying to coach and to motivate I said, "Well, let's see. How about this? I won't put any keys on it at first, but for every win we get, I'll move a key over from my current key chain—the bigger the win the more important the key I'll move. How does that sound?"

"Yeah, that'll be great, but are you sure you have enough keys for all the wins we're gonna get?" our cockiest player asked.

I showed my current key chain.

"Since I carry more keys than we have games, we can win the state playoffs and I'll still have keys to move," I explained.

So it was agreed.

The next day we won our season opener. After the game I made a big production of it.

"Congratulations, girls. We got off to a good start today, but we can play a lot better. So to represent this win, I'm going to move the key to my shed at home to the new key chain. It's not my most important key, but it's about equal to our performance today I think."

I took the key off one key chain and put it on the other.

We continued to win. We lost a few along the way too, but for the most part we were living up to our potential and maybe a little beyond. And after each game, we talked about our performance and finished with the "move the key" ceremony.

Upcoming on our schedule was Plantation High School—in my mind the biggest game of the season. My teams had never beaten them in volleyball. We had a pretty good rivalry with them in softball and had beaten them in that sport a few times, but our success had not carried over to volleyball. The team knew I wanted very much to get that monkey off our backs.

We did it. They came to our gym. We played great. We demolished them.

I had never seen a team so excited after a game.

I praised them. I lauded them. I gushed over them.

Then came the key ceremony.

"What key are you gonna move to represent this win?" they wanted to know.

"You know what? I don't think I own a key significant enough to symbolize what this win means to me."

One of the girls raised her hand.

"Yes," I said.

"I . . . uh . . . probably shouldn't tell you this . . . but, I . . . uh . . . have a *master key to the school*. Would you like that? Would that be significant enough?"

"WHAT the . . . where did you get . . . never mind . . . I don't think I want to know. But, yes, that would be great."

I had been trying to get a master key to the school for years. The administration at the time didn't want to give me one. It wasn't just me. They didn't want to give a master key to anyone who didn't absolutely have to have one. I didn't blame them. It's not good to have all sorts of keys to everything floating around. I only wanted one so I could get into the gym on Saturday mornings for practice. Several times I had asked and several times I was told, "There's a custodian here on Saturdays. He'll let you in and will lock up after you."

I took the key and moved it to the new key chain. Funny how the "world's greatest coach" had to get his first master key from a student.

. . .

By accepting the key from my player, I thought I was actually killing two birds at once. I was getting the master key, which I felt I needed, but I was also taking one from a student. The last thing we needed was for students to have master keys.

It wasn't until much later that I learned that what she gave me was *a copy* of the master key. She retained the original for herself. To this day I still have no idea where she got it.

AM I TESTING THEM OR ARE THEY TESTING ME?

Cheaters. I don't like them. No teacher does. We've all had to confront them at one time or another. Whenever I have caught cheaters, I have dealt with them. But it's how I've handled them that varies from cheater to cheater. It could be the mood I'm in, who the cheater is, or maybe even the day of the week that determines how cheaters are nailed in my class. I'm not really sure. Several instances of catching cheaters come to mind, but here are my favorites.

Unbelievably, a cheating boy, we'll call him John, was sitting in the seat directly in front of my podium. I always sit at the podium during testing because by sitting on the stool there, it puts me a little higher up and gives me a great view of the entire classroom. Evidently John thought that because he was so close to me, I wouldn't be able to see what he was doing. I knew right away he was up to no good. His eyes kept straying down between his legs. I'm sure he thought I thought he was looking at the desktop and reading the test when in reality he was looking between the bottom edge of the desktop and his stomach to a little slip of paper neatly ensconced between his legs. I could barely see the cheat sheet from my perch, but I could indeed see it.

The test was fairly long so I had time to figure out how I wanted to handle the situation. This time I decided not to call him out in front of the class...not to make a big deal of the fact I had him pegged as a cheater. Rather, I decided to handle it in a somewhat different manner. To my recollection this is the only time I ever handled a cheating incident in this way. I decided to write a note. It read:

Dear John,

You have just been caught cheating. I can clearly see the cheat sheet between your legs. You may continue to take this test if you wish, but please be advised that your grade is a zero.

Your friend,
Mr. Crosby

After completing the note, I folded it neatly four times. I got off my stool and nonchalantly strolled around the room looking every bit the proctor that I was by keenly observing the students taking their tests. As I headed back to my stool behind the podium, I passed by John's desk and simply laid the folded note on the corner of the desk.

John stared at the note for a second or two before he opened it. I watched as he read it. I saw his face turn pale. I saw him put his pencil down, fold his arms and rest them on the desk, and then place his head down on his arms. He had been nailed. He knew it. He accepted it. He never even came to me to talk about it. Nor did he ever cheat in my class again.

· · ·

Another front row cheater was a boy whom we'll call Brian. (What is it with these front row cheaters? Do they think we are blind or just plain stupid?) Anyway, Brian also had a cheat sheet tucked neatly under his leg. As he got to questions he didn't know, he would glance down to get the answers. Evidently, Brian made a move he never should have made because something caused his cheat sheet to fly out from under him and land on the floor about three feet in front of his desk. I saw it happen. I knew what it was, but Brian didn't know I knew. In his panic to cover his blunder, he did the logical thing. He slid down slightly in his seat, extended his long legs, and firmly planted his foot on top of the crib sheet. I was about to go make a big deal of it when I realized he was in what had to be the most awkward, uncomfortable position anyone could ever hope to endure. I decided to wait...to see just how long he could maintain that position. Picture him. Six feet four inch Brian slouched down in his seat with his long legs outstretched in front of him but with one foot flat on the floor to cover the sheet. I tried to position myself like that later and could only last a few minutes it was so uncomfortable, but Brian was a real trooper. He stayed in that position for at least 20 minutes. He couldn't read the sheet from where it was with his foot on top of it, but he couldn't just remove his foot either. I would see the cheat sheet if he did that. So he did the only thing he could. He finished taking the test by sitting in that horribly awkward, uncomfortable position.

When I realized he was about to finish his test, I walked over and stood in front of him. Still not suspecting that I knew anything, he handed me his test. He did not, however, move his legs. I continued to stand there. He continued to sit there in that agonizing contortion. Eventually, he tried to drag his foot toward him hoping he would drag the cheat sheet with it. But the unthinkable happened to Brian. His foot came toward him just fine, but the cheat sheet didn't. In fact, it was left right at my feet in plain sight.

I bent down and picked it up.

"Brian," I said, "this is yours I believe. And so, by the way, is this zero." I wrote a big red zero on the top of his test.

To the best of my knowledge, like John, Brian never attempted to cheat in my class again either.

. . .

Before I came to Northeast, I taught for two years at a school in Quincy, Florida. It was there that I caught my very first cheater. It was my first and has always been my favorite encounter of that kind.

This time it wasn't a test, but it was a worksheet of some sort. The margin of the worksheet was a little too close to the top of the paper, but there was ample room at the bottom for students to write their names. But, there was no name line per se.

Anyway, this stalwart lad whom we shall call Steven was far from the brightest light in the harbor. He had very little knowledge of the subject at hand so he did the only thing he thought he could to make a decent grade. He copied the paper of the girl next to him. Again, we are talking about a front row student. I'm not sure how good I have been at catching back row or even middle of the room cheaters, but I was death on those front row cheaters.

I watched intently as Steven read each question, figured out he had no idea as to its answer, and immediately turned and copied the paper of Tynecia Wilson (name changed to protect the innocent) who sat unsuspectingly beside him.

As was the case with John and Brian, I did not jump on Steven immediately. Instead, I let the scene play itself out. Eventually, he finished the worksheet (about 30 seconds after Tynecia finished hers as I recall), but not before he did something to seal his own doom. In essence, he gave me all the proof I would need to convict him of the crime of copying.

So when he came up to turn in his paper, I said, "Steve, old buddy, I can't accept this paper."

"Why not?" he asked in disbelief.

"Because you cheated," I said.

"Cheated? How did I do that?"

"Easy," I said. "You copied off her paper."

"No, I didn't," he denied vehemently. "You can't prove it."

"Oh, but I can," I said.

"No, you can't. If you could, you would have said something to me if and when you saw me do it."

"I didn't say anything, but I really do have proof."

"Show me," he said.

With that I pointed to the two words at the bottom of his paper just above his name. "You see those two words right there?" I asked him.

"Yeah, so what?"

"I hate to break this to you, but that's her name!" Clearly printed there were the words Tynecia Wilson.

"You not only copied her answers; you copied her name too! Is that proof enough for you?"

All he could say was, "Oops."

. . .

No chapter on cheating in school would be complete without mentioning the incident that, in my experience at least, wins the prize for the most ingenious. My son told me what one of his baseball teammates did in a chemistry class.

It seems that for a chemistry test an essay was given ahead of time. Students were allowed to prepare for it but were not allowed to write it up until they arrived in class. No notes were allowed. Thus all research and organization had to be done ahead of time, but no aids whatsoever could be used during the actual writing of the essay.

The teammate, let's call him Paul, went to the teacher at the beginning of the period and asked very politely if while he wrote he might possibly be allowed listen to some music through some headphones. He said it would relax him and help him to organize his thoughts more clearly. The unsuspecting teacher said he didn't mind.

Paul proceeded to play a tape, not of music, but of the answer to his essay that he had dictated very slowly on the tape the night before. A girl who had had the class in the previous year had given Paul her essay which had already been given an A grade. Paul simply read it to the tape, and as it played back the answer to the essay, he copied what he heard.

To add an air of authenticity to it all, Paul did some minor gyrations and head bobbings to make it look as if he really were listening to music.

Very ingenious, but my question is this. Why don't kids just spend their time studying instead of trying to find ways like this to avoid it?

NO WRITING ON THE FURNITURE, PLEASE!*

One of the few teachers who has been at Northeast longer than I have is my good friend Bill Tobias. Bill teaches science, and for many years we taught right across the hall from each other. Prior to that, however, Bill team taught a course or two with Linda Overgard (formerly Linda Melvin) another good friend of ours.

It seems that one day, in one of those team teaching courses, it was Bill's turn to lecture, and he was strolling around the room orating on photosynthesis or meiosis or eels or some other such soporific topic. It was a large classroom with many students, and when Bill tired of strolling, he stopped to rest. There happened to be a straight-back chair that had been put on top of a table. Bill continued to lecture as he leaned over to prop himself up on the chair.

For some reason as he placed his elbow on the chair, he glanced down at the seat of the chair. What he saw there brought an instant end to his lecture. He was almost paralyzed. He couldn't utter another syllable. No one knew what had happened. He frantically motioned for his partner Miss Melvin to come over. She hurried over to see what was up. She was concerned that maybe he was having some kind of attack—a stroke maybe. His face was contorted, and when she got to him, she saw he was absolutely shaking. It was then that she saw that the nearly paralytic state he was in was caused by . . . laughter. He was laughing uncontrollably—so hard, in fact, that it was inaudible. It was one of those laughs where you laugh so hard you lose your breath.

"What is it?" she asked anxiously.

Bill could hardly move, but he managed to point to the seat of the chair where Linda read what someone had printed in big, bold, black magic marker lettering.

"MISS MELVIN HAS BIG TITS."

Linda's eyes widened and her jaw dropped, but she did what her instinct told her to do. She immediately grabbed the chair and rushed it out of the room.

Where she took it, no one knows. We do know that it was never seen again in our school.

The person who wrote it was never caught.

To this day Bill still howls with glee every time he recalls that day, that chair, and the look on Linda's face when she read what it said.

HO, HO, HO, MERRY . . . BALDERDASH?*

Okay, we freely admit it. Most, if not all, teachers agree that one of the best things about teaching is the vacations. We deal with students 180 days a year, but have nine weeks off in the summer, two weeks off at Christmas, and another week off during the spring. Those alone account for 12 weeks of vacation, but we also get Martin Luther King Day, President's Day, Memorial Day, Labor Day, and here in South Florida we even get a couple of Jewish holidays.

The general public tends to begrudge us our free time. But what no one realizes is the day before a vacation starts can be absolute torture if not handled properly. The kids have no desire whatsoever to do any work on those days, and the administration frowns on teachers having any kind of party in the classroom. So what are we to do? Several years ago I came up with a brainstorm that has saved me many times on those vacation eves. It is called *Balderdash.*

Balderdash is a board game played by individuals. The way *Balderdash* is played normally is a word, albeit a very difficult word, is given to each of the players who in turn writes a made up definition for that word on a slip of paper. Made up? Yes. No one ever recognizes the words so the definitions have to be total creations of the imagination. Heck, I have a Master's Degree in English, and I've only heard of three of the words in the game myself.

The definitions are then handed to the reader who in the meantime has consulted the back of the card containing the words and from there has taken the real definition for the word and written it on a separate slip of paper. The reader then reads the definitions aloud including the real one, and players try to figure out which one is the true definition.

I truly love the game, and one day while I was stewing about what to do on the day before Christmas break, an absolute brainstorm hit me. I would adapt the game of *Balderdash* to accommodate teams in the classroom. Instead of giving everyone in the class the same word, I would make each row of five kids a team and give each row a different word. All members of a team or row would write made-up definitions for their row's word. I would write the actual definition just as in the real game. Then I would take up the definitions and one by one read them aloud. The real definition would be mixed in. The other rows would listen to the definitions read and each individual not on the team that wrote the definitions would vote for the definition he/she thought was correct. The more people a team fooled with its bogus definitions, the more points it would earn. But everyone who was able to pick out the real definition would win a point for his/her team. Thus, it was not

a good idea to make up totally stupid and unrealistic definitions as no one would vote for those.

The game itself is extremely fun, but I had the ace in the
hole that would very definitely make it something every kid
would want to play. That ace? Very simply it is called EXTRA
CREDIT! There is something about extra credit that moti-
vates students beyond the plausible. I have seen students sit
on their duffs for an entire marking period and do nothing . . .
literally amass no points whatsoever . . . and then go absolutely crazy in an effort to acquire a few extra credit points. All I
had to do was offer the winning team 10 extra credit points
per player, and it was guaranteed to produce serious competition among the rows/teams.

For years I employed this strategy. Everyone loved it. Everyone played hard. No one was goofy. No one acted up. After
all, this was for EXTRA CREDIT. A full 10-point prize was
at stake. (By the way, in my class during a marking period
roughly 2200 points make up the grade. To the best of my
knowledge never have 10 points of extra credit affected even
one student's grade. But, they didn't know that on *Balderdash* day so they all tried their hardest.)

At least that was generally the way it went until one day
the funniest single event in the history of my class happened.
One of the words I put on the board for one of the rows to define was the word "shittim." Yep, "shittim." It is pronounced
exactly the way it looks as if it would be–shit 'em. Shittim.

As soon as I put that word on the board for one of the rows
to define, I knew I was in trouble. There was instant laughter
just at the pronunciation of it. But when that was coupled
with the fact that maybe the funniest kid I had ever had in

any of my classes just happened to be sitting in the row that was to define "shittim" all hell was about to break loose.

Each student diligently went about the task of defining his/her row's word. Even Ryan (the funny kid) seemed to be going about his business with a seriousness equal to the magnitude of the extra credit gift that was at stake.

When the definitions were all handed in, I mixed in the real definitions for each word. Then I began to read them aloud. I did the shittim definitions. I don't even remember at this point the real definition for shittim, but I'll never forget what Ryan said it meant. His definition for the word shittim was a masterpiece. I almost couldn't get it out I was guffawing so. Finally, I managed to read it. Ryan's definition for "shittim" read, *"What the big giant did to the little man after he ate him."*

I still can't believe I read it aloud. I probably shouldn't have, but I did. Thunderous laughter reverberated throughout the classroom. It was without question the longest sustained laughter I have ever heard in school.

We laughed so loudly and so hard that the teacher from the classroom next door stuck her head in to see what was going on.

Needless to say, that definition got no votes. But no one in that row even cared. When a team loses out on extra credit and doesn't even care, you know the reason for it had to be something really, really good. It was. It definitely was.

TWIST AND SHOUT? NO—SHOUT AND RUN!

The class was sitting quietly taking a test. It was first period in the morning, which is usually before the troublemakers wake up to cause problems. My class had no troublemakers. They were an honors group and were very focused on their grades.

All of a sudden the door to my room flew open. I couldn't see who had opened it, nor did I have much chance to see.

Words were shouted into the quiet classroom followed by the pitter-patter of running feet leaving the scene.

It took a second for me to figure out what had been yelled. Then I realized it. The kid had shouted, "JERRY JOHNSON HAS A LITTLE ONE!" Now, it just so happened that Jerry Johnson was sitting in the third row and maybe old Jer did or maybe he didn't have a little one, but whether that statement about Jerry was true or not true, no vagrant was going to yell into my classroom and get away with it.

I quickly ran to the door. He had vanished into thin air. There was no sign of even a corridor door closing behind him. At that point I did something totally out of the ordinary. I left my class unattended and went to hunt him down.

Since mine is the last room at one end of the corridor, I knew he had to have gone out the doors at my end. I quickly ran through the doors. No trace of him. I took a chance and turned right. I went to the next corridor and opened the door. I had guessed correctly. As I was entering one end of the corridor, he was exiting the other. Now he was walking, but I wasn't. I sprinted down the entire length of the hallway. When I got to the end, I had another choice to make. Did he go right or left. This time I guessed left and BINGO! I saw him. He was heading out into the parking lot.

I ran up to him and took him by the arm. I said, "You really shouldn't have done that, Ace."

"Done what?" he said with absolute surprise.

"Yelled into my room that Jerry Johnson has a little one," I informed him.

"I don't even know Jerry Johnson," he replied.

"Let's go see what the dean has to say about it," I said.

Usually, at this point in a nabbing, the nabbee will cut and run for all he's worth . . . especially if the nabber doesn't know him by name. To the best of my knowledge I had never laid eyes on this child. But he didn't try to get away. He walked calmly beside me to the dean's office proclaiming his innocence every step of the way.

When we got to the dean's office, I thought luck was against me. Mr. McCoy was not in. I asked his secretary if she knew where he was and when he would be in.

"He's at the dentist's office having a root canal," she said.

Oh fine. So much for striking while the iron was hot. I really didn't know what to do next. I couldn't take him all the way over to the other side of school to see another dean . . . not with my class still sitting back in my room working on their test.

I was about to write it off to bad luck and let the kid go when the secretary said, "Vinnie is in his office if you want to see him."

Vinnie was the campus cop. He was mainly there for big arrests and didn't usually get too involved in petty stuff like this, but I thought what the heck . . . better to see Vinnie than to let this joker go completely free.

As soon as we walked in to see Vinnie, I knew I had struck oil. Before he even said hi to me, he addressed the kid.

"Hi, Ron. What have you done now?"

"So you know this cherub? I asked.

"Know him? Sure, I know him. He lives two doors down from me," said Vinnie. "What did he do?"

I told Vinnie what the boy had done and how adamantly he had denied even knowing Jerry Johnson.

When I mentioned that last part, Vinnie knit his brow.

"Of course, he knows Jerry. Jerry lives in the house between us!

Game, set, match, championship! Ron got three days of internal suspension, and I went back to check on my test takers.

Man, that felt good!!!!!

. . .

On a related note...later that day I told this story in the teachers' lounge during lunch. Jerry was only a sophomore at the time, but from that day until he graduated over two and a half years later, any time poor Jerry Johnson's name came up for any reason in the teachers' lounge, someone without fail would chime in with, "Jerry Johnson? He's got a little one, ya know!"

"DO YOU KNOW WHO I AM?"

I have never been a teacher who has wanted to spend too much extra time back at school. After putting in a full day teaching and in most years spending a couple of extra hours or so each day after school coaching, I was never very eager to go to additional functions. There is one, however, that I am very glad I attended.

It was back in the 70's. I had coached my first softball team to an 18 and 4 season and had finished second in the district. We had an excellent team and one of my players, a young lady by the name of Vicki McDonald, was selected to the first team all-county squad chosen by *The Miami Herald*.

In those days, near the end of the school year *The Herald* had a recognition ceremony for all of the players in every sport who had been selected to its all-county first team. It was held at the War Memorial Auditorium. There was no food provided, but awards were given and there was a guest speaker.

In that particular year the guest speaker was none other than the legendary basketball coach Al Maguire. When Coach Maguire got up to speak, an immediate hush fell over the auditorium. He began by telling us that just recently he had spoken at another function similar to ours but at that one there was food. He recounted an exchange he had had there with one of the service personnel.

It seems that a young rather inexperienced male about 18 or so had the job of going around to each table giving out little pats of butter to each person. When he went to the head table to give Coach Maguire his, the coach knew he would need more than he had been given so he said very politely, "I'd like another one please."

The young waiter responded, "I'm sorry, sir; I'm only allowed to give each person one."

Maguire could hardly believe his ears. In his best pull-rank voice he said, "Son, do you know who I am?"

"No, I don't," responded the lad.

"I'm Al Maguire. I'm the guest speaker here this evening. After dinner I'm going to address this entire room."

"That's great," said the boy. "I'm glad to meet you."

Then a little hesitantly the boy asked, "But sir?

"Yes," answered Maguire.

"Do you know who I am?"

Somewhat surprised Maguire said, "No, I'm afraid I don't."

The boy replied, "I'm the guy who gives out the butter, and you get one just like everybody else!"

A TRUE MEAT AND POTATOES GUY!

Okay, this didn't actually happen *in* school, but it happened because of school. That, and the fact that it still makes me smile every time I think about it, makes it eligible to be included here.

My son Andy was going to be a senior in high school. He wanted very much to have a good senior year on the baseball team because that would hopefully springboard into an opportunity to play college baseball. He had always been a good ball player but size and strength were a bit of a problem for him.

A week or so before the end of his junior year, I quizzed him about his summer plans.

"You know, Andy, summer is just around the corner."

"Yeah, I know."

"What are you planning to do besides play as much ball as you can?"

Rather than the expected, "Oh nothing much," I got this instead.

"Well . . . I was thinking . . . maybe . . . I should . . . uh . . . enroll in some kind of fitness center to see if . . . uh . . . I can put on some weight and get a little stronger before next year."

I knew Andy very, very well. For him to use that many words on something was a very clear indicator that he really wanted to do it. At the same time, I knew the hesitations in his sentence were an even clearer indicator that he really hoped I would pay for it.

His face lit up when I said, "That's a great idea! In fact, I was thinking the same thing. Got any particular place in mind?"

"There's a place called Total Wellness. It isn't that big and doesn't have all that many people working out there. I kind of thought maybe I could . . . well, we could go there first."

And so we did. I called for an appointment and the next day we went to check out the place.

The fellow in charge was a man named Gary. He was quite nice and not the least bit pushy which Andy and I both liked very much.

After a tour of the facility and a brief explanation of some of the machines that were there, Gary asked, "Why don't we go into my office, and we'll talk a little about what kind of program you want?"

When we sat down in the office, Gary began to ask Andy some questions about goals and plans and so forth, but it was the part about diet that I'll never forget. It went like this.

"So, Andy, what's your typical dinner like at home?"

"Meat . . . potatoes . . . ice tea," Andy answered while keeping with his tradition of using as few words as possible to answer questions.

"Is that it?" Gary wanted to know.

"Pretty much," Andy answered.

"How about vegetables? Do you ever eat any vegetables?" asked Gary.

"Sometimes," answered Andy, his already puny sentences becoming even shorter with each question he answered.

"What kind of vegetables?" came the next question.

"Green beans . . . corn."

"Only green beans and corn?"

"Yes."

"No broccoli, asparagus, beets, or anything like that?" Gary seemed to be trying to help Andy think of some other veggies he may have eaten at some point but had forgotten.

"No. Just green beans and corn–that's about it," Andy offered in what seemed to be a fit of wordiness.

Gary wasn't too impressed with Andy's lack of vegetables in his diet so he moved on to another food group evidently with the hope of getting a better response.

"What about fruit? Do you ever eat any fruit?"

Andy thought about it.

"No," he said.

Then after brief moment he added, *"I'm better with vegetables."*

007 COMES TO SCHOOL

Several years ago I was sitting at home one evening reading one of my favorite books. Nope, not *Gone With the Wind* . . . not *To Kill a Mockingbird* . . . not *The Red Badge of Courage* (all books one would expect an English teacher to read). This book was David Letterman's *Book of Top Ten Lists II*.

I was in the bedroom reading list after list and chuckling away. Some of those lists are hilariously funny. Evidently I had read a few too many and had made it to the point where I would laugh at just about anything because when I read the list entitled "Top Ten Ways the World Would Be Different if Everyone Were Named Phil" item number six on that list just convulsed me with laughter. I laughed so hard my sides ached. I was literally howling with delight. It was one of those snorting laughs–the kind where you try to take in air and you sound like a pig snorting. It went on for several minutes.

When I was finally able to contain myself, I went into the living room where the rest of my family was watching a DVD movie.

"Hey, pause that," I said. "You have to hear this. This is hysterical."

They were a little annoyed at the interruption but as they were always eager for a good laugh, they complied with my request.

"Okay, here's the topic—"Top Ten Ways the World Would Be Different if Everyone Were Named Phil."

They had been watching me and listening to me giggle at this book for a couple of days and were ready to be entertained themselves.

"Item number six on the list . . . get this," I said and I began to giggle again. I couldn't spit it out. Every time I tried I would get as far as "Item number six is . . . " and then uncontrollable laughter would seize me once again. There were about five false starts in all.

They looked at me in disbelief. Nothing in the entire universe could be this funny they thought. They were eager to hear it. The annoyance of the interruption of the movie was definitely gone. In its place was the annoyance of my not being able to tell what number six was because I couldn't stop laughing.

Finally, I totally composed myself. I took a deep breath. I managed to get it all the way out this time.

"Item number six on the list of 'Top Ten Ways the World Would Be Different if Everyone Were Named Phil' is '007 fans look forward to the classic line, Bond. *Phil Bond.*'"

Again I doubled over. I snorted all over again. And, as was the case in the bedroom, I was snorting alone. They all just looked at me. They weren't even smiling. They didn't think it was even remotely funny. I was in shock. This is no bunch of dead heads this family of mine. They love to laugh. They laugh easily, but this time they weren't laughing.

"You guys aren't laughing," I said.

"It wasn't funny," my 14-year-old daughter Lindy said.

"Can we get back to the movie now?" asked my sixteen-year-old son Andy.

"Mik, you thought it was funny didn't you?" I asked my wonderful wife who will laugh at just about anything.

"It was kind of funny," she said—more to humor me I think than to really admit that it was funny.

This was amazing to me. How could they not think that was funny?

"I know what I'll do," I said to myself. "I'll tell it to the gang at school tomorrow . . . the lunch bunch . . . they'll think it's funny.

We have the perfect assemblage of lunch eaters in the south teachers' lounge at my school. There are about half males and half females and all are good-natured people with good senses of humor. We tell a lot of jokes in that lounge. There is always laughter going on there. It is by far the happiest room at our school. No subject is off limits, and quite often we use each other as sounding boards for whatever the topic. Marcia Brown, Ann Cook, Kim Barron, Heather Juchemich, Chris Donahue, Janene Abrahamson, Trish Winters, Chip Shealy, Tom Popovics, Billy Strachan, Mike Collins, Dean Washburn, Pete Privitera, and Dave Hanny—they would be the jury on this. They would laugh along with me . . . guaranteed.

So the next day during lunch when all were settled in and the microwaving was finished, I started.

"Hey, you guys, what do you think of this?"

I told them the whole thing . . . how I had been reading the book and this one item just grabbed me and wouldn't turn me loose. Even then I was giggling like a silly school girl.

Finally, I got to the punch line.

Nothing. Dead frickin' silence.

Not even a grin.

It was worse than when I had read it at home. They just didn't think it was very funny.

In fact, they looked at me like I had just zoomed in from Mars. Their faces said, "How dare you bring such a stupid thing in here?"

. . .

However, in the end it was all worth it because it has turned out to be the source of much laughter ever since that day. From that day forward, anytime anyone told a joke in the teachers' lounge that was not very funny, it was inevitable. Someone would chime in with, "Bond. *Phil Bond.*"

Then there was laughter.

DON'T MESS WITH THE BACIGALUPIS

In my early days at Northeast I was given the dubious distinction of teaching the freshman gifted English class. Every kid in the class had an IQ of 130 or above. That's what it took to be placed in a "gifted" class. What they didn't tell me when they asked me to teach the class is that even though each kid was "gifted" at something, that something was NOT necessarily English. In fact, most of those kids were not English scholars.

The one thing they did have in common other than their 130+ IQ's was the support of their parents. Their parents were definitely interested in them and their success.

This manifested itself greatly at the annual Back to School Night . . . you know, the night where after teaching a long hard day of school, and, for some of us at least, after coaching a long, hard practice or game after school, we got to go back to school in the evening for another couple of hours to address the parents of the students in our classes one period at a time.

It never failed. I saw it every year I taught the gifted—especially the freshmen gifted. Whereas other periods would have maybe one parent for about every ninth kid, the parents of the gifted kids would show up in droves. Usually both parents would show up. Sometimes even a grandma and grandpa would come too. And though the gifted classes themselves were usually quite a bit smaller than regular classes, you certainly couldn't prove it by Back to School Night.

Anyway, on this one particular Back to School Night, the pattern was holding true to form. In first period I had about eight parents for 31 kids. In second period, a slow class, I had two parents for 23 kids. And so it went until the last period of the evening—the gifted period. Those parents came in waves. I had never seen so many parents in one classroom before. I tried to get their names as they came in the door. I would introduce myself, and they, in turn, would say their names and the name of their child.

"Hi. We're the Thompsons—Sadie's parents. How's she doin'?"

Luckily we were forbidden by the administration to talk about individual students and their progress. So I would have to say something like, "Oh, Sadie's a sweet girl, you must be very proud of her," even if Sadie was, for the most part, worse than a root canal.

Equally fortunate for us teachers was the 10-minute length of each period. By the time we said anything about the course and what we were doing, the period would end, and the parents would be off to the next class. So we never really had a chance to be pinned down on too much of anything.

As I recall, the gifted class that year had 17 students in it. There were 35 desks in the classroom . . . so even if each kid had two parents show up, there would have been room to accommodate everyone.

Unlike students when they enter a classroom, the parents all want to sit as close to the front of the room as possible. Students, on the other hand, always come in and head for the desks along the back wall. In fact, some see that as the only reason to get to class early. Anyway, there were just two open seats as the bell rang for me to start my 10-minute spiel.

I had just begun when two additional parents straggled into the room.

Since I had met everyone else at the door, I thought it only right that I should get the names of these parents too. So I interrupted myself in mid sentence and turned to the late entries and said, "Welcome. I'm Mr. Crosby, and you are?"

They said in unison, "We're the Bacigalupis (Batch a gal ooo peees); Michelangelo's parents."

Now, Michelangelo Bacigalupi was the most gifted of the gifted. That kid was brilliant and not just in English either. He had it together in everything he did. And that's why this next part was so stupid on my part. I still can't believe I did it. I guess it was just my jovial nature taking over. That and the fact that Michelangelo Bacigalupi was indeed so very brilliant I couldn't resist making a wisecrack.

Without batting an eyelash I said with a dead straight face, "Oh . . . I don't really know how to tell you this and probably shouldn't in front of everyone here, but . . . Michelangelo . . . is lagging behind in his work."

"He is?" Mr. Bacigalupi said in utter astonishment. Why wouldn't he be astonished? I'm sure Michelangelo had never lagged behind in anything in his entire life. Mom got an instant look of angst as well.

Then came the punch line . . . the kicker . . . the attempt at humor that I thought would be so cute.

"Yes," I said. "I think it's because I require the students to write both their first and last names on their papers, and by the time Michelangelo writes all of that the period is over."

Everyone laughed. Well, almost everyone. Count the Bacigalupis out of that group.

I don't think they were too upset. They just weren't too impressed with their son's English teacher.

Thus ended my Back to School Night comedic career. Never again did I mess with a name or even joke about a kid lagging behind.

A BAD COMBINATION?

You have to know John Lanier. He was the Modern European History teacher at our school when I started there. He also coached football. The kids loved him . . . but they were scared to death of him too. Heck, I know several teachers who were scared of him. For the first several years I taught at Northeast, I was even scared of him.

He was an intelligent man. He had a very deep voice. He had a slow, southern drawl. He had no patience with immaturity. He taught seniors. They never messed around in his class. They were never even late for it. Or if they were, it only happened once. His deep voice enabled him to command instant respect without yelling. But he was certainly capable of yelling. Every once in a while he would cut lose, and then everyone knew it was time to lie low and shut up. He was a former Marine, and it was obvious he had been tough as nails. He still was. He didn't beat around the bush either. He told you what he thought even if it might not be what you wanted to hear. He also was badly in need of a hip replacement which eventually he got after he retired.

With all that as background maybe you will understand why I so much enjoyed witnessing this next scene as it played out.

It was after school. Most of the kids had gone home, but there were a few stragglers. One of them was outside my door. I heard banging and clanging and thrashing and even a little profanity. I went to the door and opened it to see what in the world was causing all the commotion. I saw two people.

First, I saw a student abusing his locker . . . physically, verbally, completely. The kid had obviously had a bad day and was anxious to go home but needed to open his locker to either get something or to stash something before he could leave. The locker was not cooperating in the slightest, and the kid was not amused. I was about to say something to the boy when I noticed the second person.

The second person was none other than John Lanier. He had come into the corridor from the far end and was limping our way. His bad hip didn't allow him to hurry, but it did allow him to observe things completely as he hobbled along. I noticed that he too was watching the scene at hand and hearing all the racket. Rather than say anything to the boy, I thought I'd just stand there and watch to see if Mr. Lanier said anything.

He didn't disappoint me.

As he continued to limp toward us, the boy continued to pound on and yank at and bang into and swear at his locker. Lanier kept getting closer.

When he got up even with the boy, I'll never forget what he said.

*"I've got an idea, sonny. Why don't stand back over there . . .
get a good running start . . . and butt your damned dumb head
against it? That should take care of it."*

With that the boy was stunned but not really why one
would think. Most kids would apologize all over themselves,
though they wouldn't really mean it, and then much more
calmly, at least while they were being watched, attempt to
open the locker one more time. Not this kid.

Instead he hit himself on the forehead and said,
"Stupid idiot."

I immediately cringed as I thought, "OH, NO. Kid, you
aren't really that dumb I hope."

I was sure Lanier would kill the kid for calling him an idiot,
but before John could say anything, the boy quickly added,
"Sorry, sir, not you . . . me. I just figured out I'm trying to open
the wrong stupid locker."

With that he moved over to the next locker and opened it
on the first try.

Kids. Even John Lanier had to smile at this one.

"WHAT'S THE SCOOP WITH THE POOP, SNOOP?"

My dog Snoop is 11 years old. We got him when he was eight weeks old and we love him dearly. Not too long ago something happened to Snoop that worried us to death. His back legs became completely paralyzed and not only could he not walk, he couldn't even stand up.

Why is this chapter being included in a book dealing with things that happened in school you're probably wondering. I wish it had nothing to do with it. Unfortunately for me it does. In fact, it eventually led to what may have been the most embarrassing moment of my teaching career.

I went to school as usual that morning. My wife Mikki fed The Snooper as we sometimes call him and let him out the side door to take care of his business. On most days Snoop would stay out for five minutes or so, do his duty, and then bark to get back inside the house. This morning was very different.

Almost immediately after returning inside herself, Mik heard this pitiful yelp rather than the usual bark. "What in the world?" she thought.

She quickly went back outside to find Snoop completely unable to move his hind legs. He was scared and so was she. She tried to move him. He growled. She tried to pick him up. Ridiculous. The dog weighs 50 pounds. She can bench press only about 15 pounds so obviously she couldn't lift him. The fear she saw in his face and eyes made her know for certain this was a very grave situation.

All she knew to do was call me at school. The phone rang in my classroom. It was two minutes before the bell to start school. I was busy stapling tests and almost didn't answer it. I figured it was a parent with a question about the yearbook or something. Something told me to pick up the phone so I did.

It was Mik, and she was crying.

"What's the matter? I asked anxiously.

"It's Snoop. He can't move his legs, and he's too heavy for me to lift. You have to come home. He's outside by himself. I have to get back to him. Good-bye."

Wow. I didn't even have a chance to say okay. I left the room and found Lori Carlson, the closest administrator. I told her the story and that I had to go. She said she would get someone to cover my class so off I went.

When I got home, Snoop was still outside sort of under a bush. Mik was beside him, petting him, trying to make him feel as if the situation weren't desperate. I immediately picked up the pup, put him in the car, and headed to the animal hospital.

It turned out, after going to our vet, then an animal neurologist, and finally an animal therapist, that Snoop had suffered what was the equivalent of a stroke to his spinal chord. No medication or surgery could cure it; only therapy could help. We left him with the last vet for 17 days. After about 10 days of intense acupuncture, laser treatment, underwater treadmill exercise and who knows what else, Snoop began to walk again. Not great, very wobbly, but it was indeed walking.

On the 18th day we settled our bill (which brought the grand total paid to the combination of three vets to a staggering $3,600+).

We didn't care. We had The Snooper back, and he was walking again. That's what was important.

We petted him. We babied him. We pampered him. We loved him.

The first morning after we got him home, I was headed out the door to school when I noticed something out of the ordinary. I glanced at the couch and saw something brown there. No, absolutely not. It couldn't be that. Could it?

"Mik," I called. "Come here and look at this. Quick."

When Mik came in she knew exactly what it was. Snoop had somehow during the night climbed up on the couch and had laid a not so golden egg-shaped glob of poop right in my favorite television watching spot.

Thirty-six hundred dollars it cost to get this dog back home so he could poop on our sofa . . . and not just on the sofa . . . on the sofa between the cushions so it was smeared on two cushions rather than just one. Some frickin' deal that turned out to be.

Mik remained calm. She knew I had to get to school so she said, "You bring the cushions into the laundry room and go to school. I'll take care of cleaning them." Have I mentioned the woman is an absolute saint? If I didn't know it before, I certainly knew it then.

I carefully picked up the first cushion, held it arms length away from me and took it to the laundry room. Then I went back and picked up the second one, and with great care carried it to the laundry room as well.

Snoop in the meantime looked like he had just been caught with a paw in the dog biscuit box. He looked so guilty. He knew he had done wrong, but I had the feeling he really couldn't help it.

Somehow I managed to say, "That's all right, Snoop. Mommy'll take care of it," then I bolted for the door.

First period was taking a test. I didn't have to talk much. Mostly I sat behind my desk and waited for them to finish.

Second period was newspaper class, and they were all working on their articles. I spent about 10 minutes in front of the class talking and then turned them loose on their assignments.

Third period was yearbook class. I only had a few things to say to them before letting them get to work too. So altogether I had only been in front of classes for a little over 15 minutes of the 3 hours plus that had passed since the beginning of the day. (We have 90-minute class periods.)

After finishing my speech to yearbook class, I went to sit at my laptop to check some pages. That's when I first noticed it. There was a big smear of brown on my shirt a little above belly button height. What the heck is that I wondered?

And then it hit me. Oh no!! Can it be? I dashed out the door and went straight to the teacher's lounge and into the restroom. I took off my shirt. I held the spot up to my nose. There was no smell (actually there probably was, but my sense of smell has never been very good), but it had to be residue from the morning's adventure with Snoop.

I scrubbed it and scrubbed it and scrubbed it. I used regular old liquid hand soap from the dispenser and wet paper towels. It was just my luck that I was wearing a pale yellow shirt that day. The brown wanted to be a permanent decoration it seemed. Finally, after about 20 minutes of scrubbing and wiping and drying, it was mostly gone.

I went back to class. The kids were still busy doing their work. They hardly knew I had left the room. Did I get away with this completely? Did no one notice that I had been wearing dog poop all day?

No one is that lucky I thought, but maybe the good Lord was looking out for me. Maybe I had used up all my luck for the next several years and had gotten away with it.

That's what was going through my mind when Brandon, one of the yearbook kids said, "Did you have something on your shirt, Mr. Crosby?

Nuts. They had seen it. Probably everyone had seen it. They'll be telling their grandchildren about it some day. "And one day, Timmy, I had a teacher who stood up in front of our class with dog crap all over his shirt and he didn't even know it," they would say.

I responded to Brandon by saying, "I thought I did, but it's off now."

I worried about it all night. The next day I addressed each class at the beginning of the period. "Did you guys notice anything yesterday?" I asked.

They didn't know what I was talking about.

"Anything on my shirt?" I continued.

"Yes, we saw it. What was it? We thought you had spilled your breakfast on yourself."

Then I told them the whole embarrassing story.

I guess I hadn't gotten away with it after all.

TEACHERS' PETS

We aren't supposed to have pets, but all teachers have them. I know I have had several over the years. In looking back at it now, I can say that most of my "pets" were kids who were on my yearbook staff. In the first place those students were hand picked by me, and secondly we worked so hard and so closely together on the production of the yearbook that we seemed to form a great bond. In particular, my editors were really special—every one of them. To this day I still love them all and appreciate all the hard work they put in for the common good.

I always had a yearbook staff of only 12 students, and I took the absolute cream of the crop. Knowing full well that as adviser, the worse the staff I chose, the more work in the long run it would be for me caused me to make certain the ones I selected were top-notch.

Students who were yearbook wannabes had to fill out applications, get teacher recommendations, and be interviewed by me before they could make the staff. I seldom missed when it came to picking good ones.

I can remember missing on one though, and I don't mean I picked her for the staff and she was lousy—quite the contrary. She jumped through all those hoops mentioned above and seemed qualified, but I didn't have enough room on the staff to take her so she got a rejection letter.

Amazingly, she tried again the next year. It shows a lot of persistence and a lot of guts when a kid attempts something one year and is turned down and then comes right back at it the next year. That's a real positive sign, and that's what happened with Nicole. At the end of her freshman year, she applied for yearbook, didn't make it, and tried again the next year.

That second time, at the end of her sophomore year, she made it.

Once I saw her work on the yearbook and got to know what a good sense of humor she had too, I couldn't help but like her.

She evidently liked me too because on numerous occasions she said to me, "Mr. Crosby, you're the bomb!"

"Is that good?" I remember asking her the first time she said it.

"Oh, yes, it's very good," she said.

One day I must have really outdone myself because she changed her usual metaphor to, "Mr. Crosby, you are the bomb diggity!"

Though I didn't ask, I was pretty sure that meant that I had surpassed "bomb" status and had ascended at least one rung higher on the explosives chart.

Near the end of her senior year, Nicole went off to Orlando to audition to become a dancer at Disney World. She was quite nervous about it, and I couldn't resist the temptation to tease her a little.

"Nicole," I said, "I'm sure you'll do fine at your audition, but aren't you just a little worried about what will happen if you make it?"

"Huh? If I make it? Why should I be worried if I make it? I'm a lot more worried about what will happen if I don't make it."

"I've been to Disney World, you know. I've seen those dancers. Some get to be Snow White or Cinderella or Wendy from Peter Pan but some . . ." I let my voice trail off.

"Some what?" asked Nicole.

"Some end up as dancing trees. What if you make it and end up being a dancing tree? Wouldn't that worry you a little? No one will ever see your face. You'll just be out there dancing up a storm but no one will know it's you. You'll just be a tree. Good thing they don't allow dogs at Disney World."

"I'm not going to end up being a dancing tree."

"Okay, but if you do, remember I warned you."

That was about three weeks before the school year ended in her senior year, and I let very few days go by from then until the last day without mentioning the dancing tree possibility.

After she graduated, Nicole did indeed go off to Disney World to become a dancer. At the beginning of the next school year, she came back to see me. Unfortunately, I wasn't in my room at the time and didn't get to see her, but I did find the following note written on my board.

Mr. Crosby,

I came by and your [sic] not here. What's up with that? You're still the bomb dig-gity though. Just saying HI.

Nicole

P.S. I'm not a dancing tree.

THE 12-MINUTE RUN

Though I have taught at Northeast for 33 years and have coached over 30 seasons of athletics there, when my kids were attending a rival high school about two miles down the road, I did some coaching there, too.

Now that was difficult. There were times when Northeast would play a Fort Lauderdale High team that I was coaching; so after spending the day teaching at Northeast, I would go to Fort Lauderdale High to coach—sometimes *against* some of the same kids I had taught earlier in the day in class at Northeast.

Despite that, the time I spent coaching at FLHS was very enjoyable. It gave me a chance to spend some quality time with my own kids while offering the challenge of coaching at the same time.

My son Andy played four years of baseball at Fort Lauderdale High. I was there as a part of the coaching staff all four years. Baseball season was, of course, in the spring, but in the fall the high school baseball teams were allowed to have a conditioning program. They would run, hit the weight room, and, in general, do conditioning drills that would help get them ready for baseball season.

I can remember the very first conditioning session in Andy's junior year. About 20 or so players had assembled. We had directed them in some warm up calisthenics, and then Coach Portice, our head coach, had them sit in the dugout while he explained what they would be doing next.

Now, there was a player by the name of Brian Stinnet on the team. Everyone liked Brian. He was as naive as the day he was born—one of those gullible types who would believe anything. He wasn't the quickest thinker and seldom even realized when someone was putting him on. Coach Portice had known him for years and especially liked to mess with him. He was always asking him ridiculous things like, "Brian, do you walk to school or bring your lunch?"

Brian would never have an answer. He would always look puzzled, say nothing, and grin a little sheepish grin.

On that first day of conditioning when Coach Portice had the team in the dugout and was explaining the next activity, he couldn't resist asking Brian another of those preposterous questions.

We were about to embark on the infamous 12-minute run. It was very uncomplicated. Everyone would go over to the track, line up at the starting line, wait for the whistle, and then run . . . for 12 minutes. The object, of course, was not only to see who could actually run without stopping for that length of time but also to see how far individuals could run in twelve minutes. It was a gauge to see who was in shape and who needed to get in shape.

After explaining the activity but before leaving the dugout to head to the track, Portice unleashed his question to the unsuspecting Brian.

"Stinnet," he said, "how long do you think it will take you to do the twelve minute run?" Not how far do you think you can run, or do you think you can run for 12 minutes, but *how long do you think it will take you to do the 12-minute run?*

Stinnet decided to give this one a try. He didn't want to embarrass himself by saying nothing the way he usually did so he thought for a minute. Then he uttered his absolutely priceless response.

"Alone or with somebody?"

Brian Stinnet, wherever you are, thank you for being you!

"SO, THERE'S NO SUCH THING AS A DUMB QUESTION, EH?"

One of the units I used to really enjoy teaching was the one on using the dictionary. Most people think the only thing a dictionary is for is to find spellings and/or meanings of words. *Au contraire, mon frere.*

In addition to spellings and meanings, in some dictionaries at least, one can find all sorts of things. There is sometimes a listing of abbreviations; a Biographical Names section which gives info on famous people; a Pronouncing Gazetteer which gives basic information about countries of the world; a Forms of Address section; a listing of common English given names with both a Names of Men and a Names of Women section; a Vocabulary of Rhymes; a list and explanation of spelling rules; a list and explanation of punctuation rules and a list of punctuation symbols; a list of capitalization rules; a section on italicization; a list of colleges and universities in both the United States and Canada; and a myriad of tables within the dictionary itself showing everything from Roman numerals to weights and measures to the type of money used in various countries and many more.

In graduate school I had a course which met two times a week. We were given five questions on Tuesday, and we had to have them answered by Thursday. All we were told was the answers could be found somewhere in the school library. Though the class was only 50 minutes long, I can remember spending ten, twelve, and even fourteen hours outside of class trying to complete just one of those sets of five questions.

Of course, the object was to familiarize us grad students with all the different resources that were available to us in the library. Nowadays that same type of assignment would be a snap. Read the question; head for the internet; go to Google, and find it. Unfortunately, Al Gore had not yet invented the internet when I was in grad school, so the work of finding those answers was agony.

Anyway, when I looked in *Webster's Seventh New Collegiate Dictionary*, the dictionary I had in my classroom back in the 70's, I realized that I could do the same type of unit that I had been tortured with back in grad school. I would ask a series of questions (more like twelve to fifteen instead of five), and I would tell the class the answers could all be found in the dictionary. Beforehand, of course, I pointed out many of the tables and sections that could provide the answers, but by the time they received the worksheets many would have forgotten most of what I had said and would be reduced to plowing through the dictionary hoping to stumble on the answer.

The sharp ones would know right where to go to find the answers because they had listened when I alluded to it in my preliminary discussion of what could be found in the dictionary.

So when I asked a question like "If you were a blind person, how would you differentiate between a p and a q in writing?"

The index indicates that the Braille Alphabet Table can be found on page 101. Once there the answer is easily obtained.

Other examples of questions that appeared on my worksheets include:

- In the Jewish calendar how many days are there in the month of Shebat?
- Four fluid ounces would be equal to what?
- In what state would one find Elon College?
- What is the term for a wind that blows between 32 and 38 miles per hour?
- What will be the date of Easter in 1981? (Remember I was teaching this back in the 70's.)

During this unit there were five worksheets and students would move along as fast as they could. When they finished one worksheet, they would turn it in and pick up another one. At the very end of the unit as we reviewed what we had done and what would be on the test the next day, I was asked what is very definitely the exception to the axiom, "there is no such thing as a dumb question."

I had just pointed out the answer to the date of Easter in 1981 question. I showed them that the Easter Dates Table found on page 261 gave the dates of both Easter and Ash Wednesday for every year from 1962 to 1981. That's when Keith White asked his question before thinking.

"Why don't they have one of those tables for Christmas dates, Mr. Crosby?"

See what I mean about it being the exception to the axiom?

· · ·

The answers to the random questions and where each could have been found are as follows:

- Shebat has 30 days (Months of the Principal Calendars Table)
- Four fluid ounces is called a gill (Measures and Weights Table)
- Elon College is in North Carolina (Section on Colleges and Universities in the U.S. and Canada)
- A wind that blows between 32 and 38 miles per hour is a moderate gale (Beaufort Scale)
- In 1981 Easter fell on April 19th (Easter Dates Table)

And if there were a "Dumbest Questions of All Time" Table, Keith White's name would be there right beside his query about why we don't have a table for the date on which Christmas falls each year.

"KNOCK IT OFF, NOW!!"

My dad was the most gentle, most easy-going man one could ever hope to meet. He was in a good mood about 99.5% of the time. He seldom yelled or even got upset, but on those rare occasions when he did, look out.

The saying, "the acorn doesn't fall far from the tree" definitely applies here. I am exactly the same way. I think psychologists would call me passive progressive. As I understand that term, a passive progressive person lets things build and build until finally the venom of all that built up bile comes gushing out in the form of letting someone have it . . . big time.

Let's make sure we understand here. I'm not one of those constant yellers who lets someone have it every day. We all know teachers like that. Their yelling takes place so often that it becomes virtually ineffective. With me, it's more like about once or twice a semester, and it doesn't happen until I'm totally fed up. It has been a very effective classroom management tool for me. I have found that once I have vented my spleen on a class, they have been good as gold for weeks thereafter.

I didn't really know how effective it was until one day about ten or twelve years ago. The class I had right before lunch was not the best behaved ever. They certainly didn't measure up to my standards, and I was trying as hard as I could to whip them into shape without constantly screaming at them. It was one of those classes where each individual kid was an okay kid and fairly likable, but when they were all assembled together, they could be very obnoxious. Every day they seemed to try my patience more and more until one day I cut loose on them.

"KNOCK IT OFF," I screamed. "JUST SHUT THE BLEEP UP! I DON'T WANT TO HEAR ANOTHER SOUND IN HERE THE REST OF THE PERIOD. YOU PEOPLE ARE GETTING WORSE AND WORSE EVERY DAY, AND QUITE FRANKLY I'M GETTING SICK OF IT SO JUST SHUT UP!!!!!! I MEAN IT. I DON'T WANT TO HEAR ANOTHER SYLLABLE UT-TERED FOR THE REST OF THE PERIOD!" (Yes, I really did say "shut the bleep up." I actually used the word "bleep." I don't believe in using profanity in front of students so I would always use the word "bleep" whenever I really wanted to cuss the little bleeps out but knew I shouldn't.)

They instantly got quiet. There was, indeed, not another syllable uttered for the rest of the period. In fact, when the bell rang to go to lunch, most of the students said, "Good-bye, Mr. Crosby," or "Have a nice day, Mr. Crosby," or something to let me know they were sorry they had gotten on my last nerve.

When I got to lunch myself, I realized just how effective my well-timed screaming had been.

Jeannie Ketchen, my next-door teaching neighbor and one of the nicest teachers ever to teach at Northeast, came in and sat down beside me. Jeannie was so nice, in fact, that her students would sometimes take advantage of her niceness and get a little too rowdy.

Jeannie said, "Bob, I can't thank you enough."

She had me totally baffled. "What for?" I asked.

"For yelling at your class. When you cut loose on your group, you got my class quiet too. The silence was just what I needed."

A GOOD COACH KNOWS HIS TEAM

I thoroughly enjoyed my three years of coaching the high school golf team. After 35 seasons of coaching prior to taking that job, I was sure my coaching days were over. Tom Hysell, our athletic director at the time, knew I had done a lot of coaching so he asked me if I wanted to coach anything. Unbeknownst to me, he had several openings to fill.

"If the golf job ever comes open, I might consider coaching that. Keep me in mind as a last resort if you can't get anyone else," I told him.

"It's open, and it's yours," he said.

"Wait a second; don't you even want to interview anyone else?"

"Nope. We just had our interview, and you won it hands down."

He hadn't talked to anyone else, but I guess he knew that anyone who had coached for over 30 years and had never assaulted anyone and had never been written up in the paper with a negative focus would at least be worth a try. So the job was indeed mine.

That first golf season was fine. We went 14 and 5 and one of our players made the all-county team. It was a boys' team but my best player was a girl (she's the one who made all-county). Actually, we were fairly solid from top to bottom, but had some characters on the team.

One of those characters was a heavy set young man (let's call him Chris) who really could have been good had he lost a little weight. In fact, in my second year as coach, he did lose some weight and played much more consistently. My guess is he weighed 260 pounds if he weighed an ounce that first year. He would generally shoot a pretty good round but would somehow manage to mess up one or two holes to turn it into an average outing.

I think his problem was all the walking and carrying of clubs. High school golfers must walk the course. They are not allowed to have caddies, motorized carts, or even pull carts. The coaches, on the other hand, have electric golf carts so they can ride around from group to group to see how players are doing and to settle any disputes that might occur.

It never failed. Every time I would drive by Chris's group to ask how it was going, he would ask, "Have you seen the cart girl with the food?" Then he would follow that up with something like "I'm hungry. Send her over if you see her; will ya, coach?"

"Just play, Chris. We'll take care of the food later," I would usually tell him.

After seeing this phenomenon repeat itself for an entire season and part of the next season, I thought I would show off a little. We were playing two other schools on our home course at Pompano Beach Municipal. The third hole is a par three followed by a long par five dogleg to the left. My fellow coaches and I, each in a separate cart, were parked behind the third green in the rough of the fourth hole. We were about a hundred yards or so from the fourth tee and pretty well out of the line of fire on the tee shots.

My boy Chris was on the tee, and, as usual, ripped his drive. It went sailing way over our heads and landed another 150 yards or so down the rough. Chris would have to walk right past us to get to his ball.

I said to the other coaches, "Watch this. When this kid walks past, I guarantee he'll say something about the cart girl or food or something to that effect."

"Does he always do that?" one of the coaches asked.

"Every time," I replied.

Chris was about up to where we were sitting by that time. He must have been deep in thought as he passed by us because he said nothing. Nary a syllable came out of his mouth. He just kept walking toward his ball. I gave him plenty of time. He was a good 40 yards beyond us. This was ridiculous. He always asked something about the whereabouts of the cart girl. I was about to offer up some excuse to the other coaches—something like "it's early yet; he's only on the fourth hole," or "I think I saw him finishing off a pizza before he teed off"—anything to make me not look quite so stupid.

Good old Chris—dependability is a wonderful trait. Before I could say anything to my coaching compadres, Chris turned around and yelled from about 50 yards away.

"COACH, CAN YOU GET THAT CART GIRL OVER HERE? I'M STARVING!"

Pride swelled in me. I remembered reading once, "Good coaches always know their players." I'm sure predicting when players will ask for food was not what the quote had in mind, but it sure made me feel good. Atta boy, Chris.

OGDEN NASH TO THE RESCUE

Saturday. It's every teacher's favorite day of the week. It's a day to relax, to let energy refill, to enjoy time away from school and the kiddies.

Unfortunately, not every Saturday is like that. In fact, there was one Saturday in particular that was just the opposite of that for me. I, along with fellow teachers Bill Tobias and Linda Overgard, for what must have been some completely idiotic reason, which I don't even recall anymore, signed up for a Saturday training session at a local high school. It was held in the school library and that, in retrospect, is the only thing that saved us.

There were about 40 or 50 teachers from all over our county packed into the library where the training was supposed to last from 8:30 a.m. to 5 p.m. with an hour off for lunch. At first it was okay, but as time wore on, the session became more and more tedious. Drudgery, sheer unadulterated drudgery, is how I would describe the last seven hours of the day. In other words, the first half hour and lunch were fine, but the rest of it was the American version of Chinese water torture.

We did some useless and completely meaningless group exercises but mostly we sat and listened to the person in charge—one rather rotund individual named Dr. Joe Hillery. Dr. Hillery was jovial and good-natured enough, but his attempts at humor fell way short on the laugh meter especially on a Saturday morning.

By 2:30 that afternoon Bill, Linda, and I were dying. My jaws were sore I had yawned so much. One look at them told me they were as worn out from ennui as I was.

It was desperation I guess that made me seek a diversion—any kind of diversion—to help me get to 5:30. 5:30!!!!! Yikes, it was three full hours away.

I glanced at the shelves in the library. With just my luck we were seated next to the poetry section. Now, I like poetry. I teach it to my English classes, but Shakespeare's sonnets and/or Robert Frost's "Mending Wall" were not exactly what I needed right then. But hark!!! Something of interest caught my eye. A volume of Ogden Nash poems nearly jumped off the shelf at me. I love Ogden Nash. Some of his poems are very funny. He was just what I needed right then—anything to help me tune out old Dr. Joe who continued to ramble on up front.

I opened the volume. The first poem I saw was one I had never read before. It was extremely short. It was typical Ogden Nash. I love the way he adjusts the spellings and pronunciations of words to fit his purpose. He had done it to perfection in this poem, and it struck me so funny.

The poem was called "Geographical Reflections." It simply said:

The Bronx?
No thonx.

I started to giggle. It hurts when you want to and need to laugh out loud but can't because the room is quiet and you can't disturb what's going on there.

Bill and Linda were seated directly across from me. They saw me straining to keep myself quiet. They wanted to know what was so funny. I passed the book across the table. They read the poem. It struck them as funny as it had struck me. In reality the poem isn't that funny, but given the situation we were in, we would have laughed at someone mowing grass. They kept the book on their side of the table and continued to look through it.

I wanted it back but didn't really need it because that one poem had inspired me. I knew what to do. I decided to write my own poem. Yep, that's what I would do. In fact, I would write it about our teacher for the day–Dr. Joe Hillery. He was about as juicy a topic for a poem as anyone could ever hope for. His large pot belly, his attempts at humor–what else did I need? I began to write in the style of Ogden Nash. I wrote:

The Prof
by Ogden Crosby

Our teacher, one Dr. Joe Hillery,
Tells jokes which are really quite sillery.
Though humor he lacks,
He loves lunches and snacks
Which is evidenced by his pants which he fillery.

Upon finishing my masterpiece I passed it across the table. Bill and Linda read it. Then they had my problem—how to laugh their heads off without making a sound.

At the end of the seminar, we were to write an anonymous critique of the day's activities. I almost submitted my poem and let it go at that, but I didn't. Dr. Joe seemed so proud of his work, I didn't have the heart to tell him how we really felt. Besides, he meant well.

Anyway, that was over 20 years ago, and I have not been to a Saturday seminar since.

. . .

Not too long ago I was telling my friend Chip Shealy about the incident, and I bet him that if he went up to Bill Tobias and mentioned the Bronx, Bill would respond with "no thonx." Sure enough. Chip saw him that afternoon and out of the clear blue said, "Hey, Bill, I've been meaning to ask you what you think of the Bronx."

"No thonx," Bill responded with a grin.

Death, taxes, and no thonx to the Bronx from Bill Tobias, those are the only sure things in life.

PLATO, ANYONE?

Of all the teachers I know who didn't go to Harvard, Rosemary Timoney is definitely the most intellectual. At our school she taught AP English, all the smart seniors, and was the director of the school's Gifted Program.

One day she came to me and said, "The administration told me I could select anyone in the English Department to teach the gifted freshman English class, and I think you would be perfect for the job."

This floored me. Me teach the gifted? The gifted generally comprised the upper five percent of a graduating class whereas I had barely finished in the upper 50% of mine. And now I was to teach them?

"Why me?" I asked.

"Because I know you will do a good job," was her only reply.

What did that mean I wondered? Had everyone else turned her down? Could she not think of any specific reasons to give in answer to my question so she hit me with that "you'll do a good job" line? Whatever the reason, the next year I found myself teaching the gifted freshmen.

Rosemary and I had had a conference at the end of the previous school year. She told me I could do whatever I felt they needed most—grammar, literature, vocabulary—it was totally up to me. I could even select the books that we would read. She would NOT be looking over my shoulder. I had the ball, and I was to run with it.

It took me about three minutes on the first day of school to determine that as smart as they were, there was an equal amount of immaturity to go along with it. Man, they were childish. They needed to do some growing up, or they would drive me crazy. I made an instant decision. Their first book would be *The Pigman*.

I love *The Pigman* by Paul Zindel. It is all about growing up and accepting responsibility for one's actions but that lesson is driven home amid the high jinks and hilarity interwoven throughout the plot. Even if kids missed the point of the book (which they never did because I made sure they got it), they still enjoyed the laughs. *The Pigman* was always good for laughs.

Honestly, *The Pigman* is the one book I could teach to any level. The really slow kids loved it, too. In fact, I've never heard a kid, smart or not so smart, say at any point during the reading of the book "This book is stupid." Someone always said, "This book is stupid," for every other book I've ever assigned—but not *The Pigman*. In this day and age when kids really don't like to read, the fact that no kid ever said, "This book is stupid," about *The Pigman* is truly remarkable.

Even adults I know who have read *The Pigman* love it. Well, all adults except one. Yep, you guessed it. Rosemary Timoney did NOT love *The Pigman*. Of course, she knew the theme, but didn't think it was something the gifted needed. So when she heard I was teaching it to the gifted freshman English class, she was a little perturbed. We had another conference.

"I know I said you could teach anything you wanted, but I had no idea you would resort to *The Pigman*. There are so many other books they could be reading that would stretch their minds so much more than *The Pigman*," she said firmly.

"Yes, I know," I replied. "But there is such an immaturity problem I thought *The Pigman* would be really good for them."

"Since you are right in the middle of it, go ahead with it, but promise me you won't teach it to the gifted again next year."

"I won't," I promised, all the while thinking maybe Rosemary would get fed up with me, can me from teaching the gifted altogether, and then I wouldn't have to worry about it "next year."

That didn't happen. I taught the gifted until Rosemary transferred to another school in our county a few years later.

. . .

So where's the funny part to this story? It didn't happen until after Rosemary left for her new school. She had the same job description there that she had had with us—she taught the AP kids, had the honors senior English classes, and was the director of the Gifted Program.

Evidently as she was about to embark on the teaching of Plato's *Republic* she discovered she was a few copies short of having enough to give one to each student. She wrote a note to our English Department.

Friends:

I'm ready to start teaching Plato, but do not have enough copies of 'The Republic' to go around. If you can spare any at all, please send them to me.

Thank you very much.
Rosemary Timoney.

Even though it was not sent to me, I saw the note and I couldn't resist. I wrote her back immediately,

Dear Rosemary:

I couldn't find any extra Platos but will these do for a substitute? Hope you can use them.

Bob

Of course, I enclosed three copies of *The Pigman*.

. . .

I didn't see or hear from Rosemary for a long time after that. I wondered how she had received my little joke. Would she be upset?

Eventually I saw her again—at a retirement dinner for a colleague, I believe. Much to my delight, she was still laughing about *The Pigman* books I had sent her.

Even Rosemary had to agree *The Pigman* really is good for laughs.

MAN, THAT GULF STREAM IS FAST!

Sometimes we teachers do things just to entertain ourselves. We have to have some fun; and though we never mean it to be malicious, sometimes the fun is at the expense of a student. What I am about to relate in this chapter was done all in good fun. It was not meant to hurt anyone and, in reality, it didn't. I just wish I had kept my big mouth shut.

Bill Tobias, our marine biology teacher, was teaching his class about the Gulf Stream. Part of his unit called for each member of his class to make a self-addressed, stamped post-card (with the student's name but the school's address) and put it inside a bottle. Each postcard requested that the finder of the bottle (who it was assumed would also be the reader of the postcard) fill out the card and put it in a mail box. The part to be filled out asked a) the date and time the bottle was found; b) where the bottle was found; and c) the circumstances surrounding the finding of the bottle (i.e., while swimming, boating, walking along the beach, etc.) All the bottles were to be taken by boat way out in the ocean and thrown overboard into the Gulf Stream. Then the students would simply wait for the return of their postcards and a chart would be made of the locations and times the bottles were found.

The day before the bottles were to be thrown overboard I moseyed into Bill's classroom after school. I saw all the bottles and asked about the project. He explained it to me. Immediately I had an idea for a little fun.

"Bill," I said. "Don't you have Marcy Connors in your marine bio class?"

"Yes, she's a great girl, a little gullible but a great girl."

Amazingly, Bill's description of Marcy was exactly how I would have described her. Well, almost. The key word though had to be gullible. I had had Marcy in SAT Prep the year before and knew her to be sweet as honey but more than a "little gullible" as Bill had said. In fact, on a scale of one to ten on the gullibility chart she was at least a twelve!

"Any chance we could have a little fun with Miss Marcy?" I asked.

"What did you have in mind?" Bill wanted to know.

"You know how Jim Ketchen (another teacher friend of ours) told us his neighbor is going to Portugal in a day or so?"

"Yeah, so?"

"Well, why don't we take Marcy's card out of the bottle, fill the information out ahead of time, give it to Jim to give to his neighbor, and just have the neighbor mail it from Portugal?" I asked not really thinking Bill would go along with it.

He loved it. "Great idea!!" he exclaimed.

He gave me Marcy's postcard. On it I filled in a bogus date and time when the bottle would be found. I filled in Lisbon, Portugal, as the location. And for the circumstances under which the bottle was found I wrote the following note:

Mi nombre es Carlos, and I find your bottle wash up on the beach here in Lisbon. I step on it and cut my foot. I say "Carumba, what is this?" I almost throw it back into the sea when I see a card inside. As you see, I fill it out with the date and the time and the place where I find it. If you really from Florida in the United States of America, I hope you get this back. Portugal is mucho distancioso from there.

Your new amigo,
Carlos Manuel Diego Ortega

As the days passed, more and more postcards were returned. Most of them came from Delray Beach, a small coastal community a few miles north of us. A very high percentage of the cards were returned in just a few days. Marcy still had not received hers.

On the twelfth day it came. The postcard had arrived from Portugal. When Marcy came to class that day, Bill handed her the card.

"OH MY, GOSH! MR. TOBIAS, MY BOTTLE WENT ALL THE WAY TO PORTUGAL!!!! Marcy gushed.

Bill didn't have the heart to tell her. She seemed so proud that her bottle had somehow separated itself from all the others and floated all the way to Portugal some 4,000+ miles away. Her euphoria got in the way of her sense. Why couldn't she reason it out? Her postcard had made it back in just 12 days. Why didn't she do some figuring? Surely she knew a postcard from Portugal would take at least five, six or maybe even ten days or more to get back to the USA. If it only took four days, which was virtually impossible, that would mean her bottle would have made it to Portugal in eight days! Four thousand miles in eight days? That's 500 miles a day! It could have gotten caught in a typhoon and not traveled anywhere near that fast.

But then when she didn't figure it out from the 500 miles a day, why didn't she figure it out from the note? After all, it was written with a combination of a little Spanish and some very broken English. Doesn't everyone know they speak Portuguese in Portugal?

Andrew Lynn and Hays Arnold, the two sharpest kids in the class, figured it out immediately.

"How fast did you say that Gulf Stream travels, Mr. Tobias?" one of them asked with a raised eyebrow.

Bill put a finger to his lips as if to say, "You know it isn't possible, and I know it isn't possible, but don't ruin it for Marcy."

Much to their credit they didn't say a word. No one did.

Marcy graduated with the knowledge that she had the only bottle that had somehow escaped the mundane shores of Delray Beach and had made it all the way to Europe.

. . .

I am sorry to report that it was I who eventually broke Marcy's bubble on this. Three or four years later I was in the local mall doing some Christmas shopping when I happened to bump into Marcy. During the course of the conversation I let the cat out of the bag.

I said, "Marcy, I probably shouldn't tell you this, but remember that postcard you got from Portugal when you were in Mr. Tobias's class?"

"Yeah. I still have it," she said.

"Well, it uh . . . came from Portugal all right . . . but . . . uh . . . I'm Carlos Manuel Diego Ortega. I wrote it up ahead of time, and we sent it to Portugal by way of Mr. Ketchen's neighbor who mailed it back from there. We were going to tell you about it when it came back, but you were so excited we didn't have the heart to do it."

"Darn," she said. "I wish you hadn't told me. I'm glad you didn't tell me then though; that would have been much worse."

"We thought so too," I agreed.

Too bad I had to open my big mouth. I wish we had never told her.

UNDER THE KNIFE

Coaching volleyball for 12 years was a lot of fun. Not only did I enjoy the competition of game days, I also enjoyed the opportunity to actually play volleyball myself at practices. After warming up each day with some stretching, conditioning, and calisthenics, we would do several drills, work on our serving, and finish off the practice with an hour-long scrimmage. Is it called a scrimmage even if it isn't football? I don't know. At any rate I would put my best players on one side of the net and my substitutes on the other, and we would compete. I always played with the substitutes. I'm no Karch Kiraly, but I was better than most of the players on my first team; so by playing with the subs it evened up the teams a little.

There was really only one drawback to that plan. I did not have high school knees at that point; in fact, even though I was only in my thirties, they felt like fifty-year-old knees. Every day after practice my left knee would stiffen and swell.

When it began to hurt during practices, I decided to have it checked out. Of course, I reported it to the school secretary and got a list of workers' comp. doctors from which to choose.

I didn't know anyone on the list so I chose one located close to school. The preliminary check up and x-ray determined that I had torn meniscus at the very least. It was decided that I would have arthroscopic surgery to correct it.

The day was set. It was Friday, October 14th, as I recall. We chose that day for a couple of reasons. First and foremost it was available to the doctor, and secondly it was a teacher-planning day at school. I wouldn't be missing an actual teaching day—no sub plans to worry about; no getting things together for someone else to supervise my classes. Any teachers who may be reading this know very well that quite often it's more work to get things ready for a sub than it is to just go teach it yourself. So I was happy that my knee was being done on a teacher-planning day. The only drawback was it was also pay day. Since I did not have direct deposit, it was imperative that my wife pick up my check from school.

The plan was made. I had to be at the hospital by 9 a.m. Mikki, my wife, would go with me to the hospital, wait until they took me in for the surgery, head for school to pick up my check, go to work for a couple of hours, and then return at about 1 p.m. to pick me up.

All went according to plan. I liked the doctor very much—had complete confidence in him . . . until my follow-up visit to his office the next Tuesday that is. Then I learned that he had done something I had never heard of any doctor doing before, and it made me wonder about his thoroughness.

I did have to take a day off school on the following Tuesday to hobble in to the doctor's office for my follow up appointment. I was anxious to talk to him to find out just how bad my knee had been. When I had regained my senses on surgery day, he was not there so I had not been able to talk to him about it then.

As soon as he came into the room that Tuesday, I hit him right away with, "Hi, doc, how was my knee?

"Your knee was a mess; didn't your wife tell you?" he wondered.

"My wife?"

"Yes, your wife. After I finished your surgery, which took a little longer than I anticipated, I went out into the waiting room and told your wife all about it."

"Are you sure?" I questioned.

"Sure I'm sure. Why?" he asked with a puzzled look on his face.

"Well, it's just that my wife . . . wasn't there. She had to go to school to pick up my check and then to work for a couple of hours. There is no way it could've been my wife."

He scratched his head as if trying to recall.

Then he said, "Well, I told *somebody's* wife about your knee. Come to think of it the woman did have a bit of a funny look on her face. Poor lady. Her husband was probably in for a gall bladder operation or something, and here I was telling her about *your* knee."

A few seconds passed. Then we both broke into hysterics.

IT'S FUN TO PUN BUT SUBLIME TO RHYME

I'm silly. I know it. Everyone who knows me knows it, too. I am 59 years old, but that doesn't stop me from being silly. Not only will I openly admit it, I'm proud of it.

It even helps me in class at times. For example, if I'm calling a list of spelling demons to the class to see if they can spell them correctly I'll put the word into a sentence to give an example of usage. Not always, but quite often it is a silly sentence. One that readily comes to mind is the sentence I use for the word "cemetery." For years whenever I called that word to be spelled, I followed it with the sentence, "People are dying to get into the cemetery."

Another is the word "succeed." Rather than saying something mundane like, "Do you plan to fail or succeed?" I would usually say, "He planned to eat like a canary and 'suck seed." Then after the groaning of the students died down, I often gave a more suitable example for the word which was usually that mundane sentence mentioned above "Do you plan to fail or succeed?"

Worse than that quirk, my mind is one of those that has to rhyme things. For years I have entertained myself, if not others, by making little rhymes with words. For example, on vocabulary test days in my English class, before testing students' mastery of definitions and their ability to properly use the words in sentences, I tested the spelling of the words by calling the words individually so the students could attempt to spell them. If, for example, the word "vacillate" appeared somewhere among the words on the list, I always made it number eight so I could say, "Oh great! Number eight . . . is vacillate." Idiotic I know, but as I said, I can't seem to help it.

It's not just in class that this phenomenon occurs either. Sometimes weird rhyming thoughts just come to me out of the blue. One day I was just sitting doing nothing when the strangest thought zoomed into my head. What if the then President of France met Andy Griffith and the two of them hit it off and collaborated to produce a new timepiece? They could call their creation the Jacques Chirak Matlock Clock. In fact, if it became a sought after item, people would be going into stores everywhere asking, "Do you have the Jacques Chirak Matlock Clock in stock?"

Quite often I keep these little rhyming gems to myself, but occasionally I share them with my colleagues. I was so proud of the Jacques Chirak Matlock Clock concoction that I had to share it with my lunch buddies.

One day when there was a definite lull in the lunch table conversation I asked "Hey, you guys, do you know what you would get if Jacques Chirak met Andy Griffith, and they collaborated to create a new timepiece?"

Of course they didn't know. I'm not sure they wanted to know either but one of them was nice enough to say, "No, what would you get?"

"You would get a Jacques Chirak Matlock Clock," I offered.

Needless to say there were more snickers and groans than guffaws. Actually, it was about 18 to zip in favor of the snickers and groans.

Knowing me the way they do, Chip Shealy seemed to be speaking for the group when he observed, "You made that up yourself didn't you, Bobby?"

"How did you know?" I asked.

"How do you come up with this stuff?" someone else wanted to know. No, I felt certain no one really wanted to know. It was just a rhetorical question, but I chose to answer it.

"Believe it or not, it just comes to me. It's like I'll just be sitting there daydreaming and out of nowhere these wild rhyming thoughts will come flying into my head and penetrate my brain," I replied trying to describe as accurately as possible the way these things actually did occur to me.

Without a moment's delay, it was Mike Collins who asked a very pertinent question.

"Have you considered wearing a helmet?"

I hadn't, but maybe I should.

I CAUGHT HIM WITH HIS PANTS DOWN

There aren't many sports I don't enjoy. Bowling, however, is one of the main items on my "I'd rather mow the grass than . . ." list. Actually, bowling itself is okay. I like to bowl . . . about once every three to five years.

When my kids were young, ages nine and seven or so, we used to pick up grandpa and go over to the lanes on a Saturday afternoon to bowl a couple of games. That was really fun. But being in a bowling league a few years later wasn't.

My brother-in-law was on a team that needed a fifth player so he asked me. I said, "Sure, why not?"

Well, why not turned out to be about 20 reasons not the least of which were a) the league went from September to May—every Tuesday night; b) it started at 6:30 p.m. (and some nights I didn't get finished coaching until 6 p.m. or after; so I would either be late which ticked off my teammates or I bowled without having had dinner which ticked me off); and worst of all c) I came home reeking of cigarette smoke every Tuesday night for nine months, and I DON'T EVEN SMOKE! Do you know how unwanted you feel when you walk into your own house and your own generally loving children greet you every Tuesday night without fail with, "Ewwwwwwwwwww-wwwwwww, you stink, Dad."

Now that I look back on it though, maybe it was a good thing. Maybe because they were so disgusted by the smell of stale cigarettes being brought into their house every Tuesday night that to this day neither of them smokes, and they are now 27 and 25 years old.

Anyway, one Tuesday night between games, I had to go to the restroom. I quickly ran from my lane all the way down to the other end of the building where the restroom was located. I burst into the restroom and hurried directly to the urinal. As I stood there, I looked at the guy standing at the urinal next to mine and made a startling discovery. He was a former student of mine. He recognized me about the time I recognized him. Well, he sort of recognized me, that is.

"Hey, I know you from somewhere; don't I?" he asked.

"I would think so. After all, I was your English teacher for your entire sophomore year."

"Oh yeah," he said as the light seemed to come on dimly in his head. "You're Mister . . . uh . . . Mister . . . wait, don't tell me; I'll get it."

"Well, while you're trying to remember me, let me see if I can tell you about you. You're Joe Mason; you were in my fourth period sophomore English class; you sat in the very first seat in the middle row in my room which at that time was room 25S. You made C's and D's for the most part. Your English grade could have been better, but you never once read a book for any of the four book reports I required the class to write during the year, and that tended to bring your grade down each marking period."

Now, generally I'm not able to do that regarding former students, but for some reason Joe had stuck in my memory. I rattled this information off as if it had all happened the previous month. In reality, old Joe had been out of school for three or four years which means that it had been six or seven years since I had taught him as a sophomore.

"Yeah, I remember it now. Yeah, that's it. You're Mister . . . uh . . . Mister . . . uh."

We had both finished our business at the urinals by this time, and I needed to hurry back to the lane. As I washing my hands, I couldn't resist letting Joe know that I was not impressed with his memory skills.

"Wait a minute," I said. "Let me see if I have this right. I taught you seven years or so ago. That year and every other year since then I've taught 150 students—some 1000+ students in all—and not only can I remember your name but also I remember what period I had you, your grades in my class, and even your aversion to book reports while you, who had maybe 6 teachers a year for a total of 24 or 25 in your whole high school career, can't even remember my name. Is that about the way she shapes up here?"

It was obvious from the way I had summarized the situation that I had caught Joe with his pants down in more ways that one.

"Well," Joe stammered, "you're starting to come back to me . . . yeah, that's it . . . you're Mr. Shealy."

"NOT!" I said as I opened the door.

"Hold it; aren't you even going to tell me who your are?" asked a more than a little befuddled Joe Mason.

"If you really want to know, you can look me up in the year-book," I said as I headed back to bowling.

I doubt if he ever did.

SHOW ME YOUR PENCIL

I've been teaching a long time, but I'm not totally set in my ways. In other words, when I hear about something another teacher does that sounds good to me, I steal it. I incorporate it into my own classroom technique and management.

One of the best examples of this is my seating arrangement. I attended a Back to School Night at my kids' school a few years ago, and my son's math teacher explained how he handles seating.

"I arrange seats according to grades. The A students sit in the back; the B's, C's, D's move progressively toward the front, and the F's sit in the very front row."

I liked it. I stole it. So now in my classroom students are seated alphabetically for the first marking period, but on the first day of the second marking period their seats are changed so those who made the A's in the first quarter are seated in the back and those who failed are right up front—you know, where they can hear me better and where I can step on their feet if they doze off.

When something really irritates me, I try to come up with a remedy that will dissuade that type of behavior. My belief is students need to be in class much more than they need to be going to the restroom or going out for a drink of water. What I have found to be the case, is students set it up with their friends in other classes to have to go to the bathroom at a certain time, and then when that time comes, each kid asks his teacher if he can go. Then they meet and hang out for ten minutes . . . more if they think they can get away with it. To rectify this behavior I give each student a hundred free points . . . not extra credit . . . but like a test grade of 100. But each time a kid is absent, tardy, sleeping, eating in class, or out at the bathroom, I subtract points from the free one hundred. It's all well explained to the students ahead of time. They know how much is subtracted from that free one hundred in any given circumstance. They quickly realize that if they can show up on time, hold their bodily functions, and stay awake they can enhance their grades. So when a kid asks me if he can go to the restroom, my answer is simple, "Sure, can you afford it?" That way they only go if they really have to go. As a result, I don't have to worry much about attendance, tardies, or unnecessary restroom trips.

Another thing that used to really bother me was kids showing up without a pencil on test day when they had a scantron test which is only readable if done with a #2 pencil. How in the world are they going to take the test without a pencil? They could borrow one, but that always irritated me too so I made it a 25-point penalty to *lend* a pencil. Yes, I said lend.

Let me tell you no kid likes any other kid enough to forfeit 25 points on a test just so that second kid can have a pencil.

For any student who doesn't bring a pencil, I make him go out and get one. Where? I don't care; that's his problem. Hopefully, while out without a pass, he will run into security and get a detention too. No, I'm not a vindictive sort. I just feel that failure to accept one's responsibilities should have definite consequences.

As out of the ordinary as this procedure of sending kids out to obtain pencils when they forget them sounds, I have only had a problem with it once. It has greatly enhanced students' abilities to remember to bring the proper utensils. That one time, however, was very . . . well . . . interesting.

The boy's name was Jack. He was in my regular English class, and he wasn't doing very well. He was lazy, not stupid. It was test day, and before the test was to begin I took what I like to call my "pencil survey."

"Okay, row one hold up your pencils," I would say. With that each student would show me his pencil, and I would move on to check rows two, three, four, and five. Any students without pencils would be asked to go get one.

When I came to Jack's row, he was the only one without a pencil. "Hit the road, Jack," I said. I remember thinking, "hey that's funny . . . hit the road, Jack . . . that's a song title."

Well, Jack hit the road all right. He must have been familiar with the words to the song too because he didn't "come back no more, no more, no more, no more" . . . until the next quarter. I didn't see that boy again for five weeks.

The first day of the next marking period in walked Jack.

"Man, there must be a real shortage of pencils out there," I said to him.

"No, I knew I was failing, and I knew even with a pencil I was going to fail that test too so I decided to just stay home an extra hour each day so I could get my mind right for this quarter."

It must have worked. Jack passed the next nine weeks. He also never got caught without a pencil again.

"YOU CAN'T GO ANYWHERE WITHOUT SEEING A STUDENT."

My wife continually tells me, "You can't go anywhere without seeing a student you had before, you have now, or someone who is a friend of someone who once had you for a teacher."

It's true, too. Whether it's the grocery store, a restaurant, or even church there is usually some child or former child who either had me or knows me as a teacher. Heck, I even went to a different drug store to get my first Viagra prescription filled just so I wouldn't have the Walgreen's pharmacy technician, who happened to have been a former student of mine, know I needed Viagra. (Oops, I guess she knows now if she reads this. Oh well, Walgreen's is closer anyway.)

The point is that in most instances seeing former students is rather harmless. We teachers don't go many places, if any, where we don't want to be recognized. Other than the Viagra from Walgreen's situation, I can only think of one other instance where I wanted to hide from a student. That's what this chapter is all about.

When I turned 50, I went for a physical. My doctor did the blood work and the chest X-Ray and the EKG and took all the specimens you can name. Everything was fine, but because I was 50, he uttered the dreaded C word.

"Yes, Bob, everything looks good, but you really need a colonoscopy. Everyone should have one at age 50. I don't expect they'll find anything, but if they do, it could save your life."

Never having even considered a colonoscopy before, I asked for more details. Doc told me what it was and that it was necessary but wasn't urgent. Since it wasn't urgent, I decided to wait until summer.

In June, when it was time to get out of school, I called the specialist my doctor had recommended to me. Man, those colonoscopies must be popular things. I couldn't get an appointment until late August. I would already be back in school by then.

When I went for my appointment, I filled out a questionnaire, and when I met the doctor, he gave me a rundown on the procedure.

He was very soft spoken and very reassuring, but when he laid out the plan, despite his easy going nature, I got a queasiness in my stomach that made me want to run to the bathroom right then.

He said, "The day before we do this, you'll drink a bottle of something that will clean you out. You'll spend a lot of time in the bathroom. You can only drink clear liquids and you can't eat anything solid from 2 o'clock on on that day. Then the next morning you'll come to the hospital in the morning, and you'll be in and out within a couple of hours or so. Do you have any questions?"

"Well, yes. I will be put to sleep while you do it; won't I?"

"Not completely. We'll give you something to put you into a little twilight, but you won't be completely asleep."

"Can I be?" I wanted to know. "Seems to me I might like it better if I don't know what you're doing back there."

"No, you'll be fine," he said. "You'll hardly know I'm even doing anything."

With that he sent me out to the receptionist to set up a date and time for the procedure.

"How does October 19th sound?" was the question the receptionist asked me.

October 19th! Two full months and then some away! Great. I would have to sit around and fret and dread this thing for over two months.

"Don't you have anything sooner?"

"No, I'm sorry. That's the first available day he has."

"Okay. Put me down for it," I said in my glummest voice.

The dread and depression were already setting in.

She gave me a list of instructions and I left. "This is going to be horrible," I remember thinking as I drove home."

For the next several weeks I tried not to think about it. Every once in a while though it would cross my mind, and instantly I would break into a cold sweat. I didn't know what I dreaded most. Was it the thought of someone poking around in my behind? Was it the thought of not eating solid foods for a full day? Was it the time I was destined to spend in the bathroom? All of the above seemed to be the correct response here. And then an even worse thought crossed my mind. What if he actually finds something wrong in there? What then? Will I need butt surgery? Will I ever eat solid foods again? My gosh! The negative thoughts just kept on coming.

Eventually the long awaited and long feared week arrived. It was in my thoughts seemingly 24 hours a day all week. Even sleep provided no respite. I dreamed one night that a man in a surgical mask was chasing me with a long knife. He kept saying, "This won't hurt . . . you'll be in a little twilight, remember?"

The size of the knife he was carrying made me think I was in the frickin' twilight all right . . . the Twilight Zone!

Two o'clock on the day before my procedure arrived. I knew it would. Secretly I think I had hoped it never would arrive. I had last hour planning; so I left school a little early to drink the medical version of Draino which was going to "clean [me] out" as the doctor had said.

Man, he wasn't kidding when he said I would log quite a bit of bathroom time.

The next morning arrived. We went to the hospital. I was as nervous as a cat in a room full of rocking chairs. We sat in the waiting room for what seemed like an eternity.

Finally, "Mr. Crosby," a nurse called.

"Here," I said and stumbled as I got up.

"Go right through those doors, and they'll get you ready."

They had their work cut out if they were going to get me ready. I was about as unready as anyone could be.

When I got into the holding room, they gave me one of those backless gowns and put me into a rolling bed where I was to "relax." Fat chance.

I was freezing. My teeth were chattering I was so cold.

But then the worst thing of all happened. Yes, the worst. Worse than all the dread, all the fear, all the no eating, all the toilet time I had logged, all the everything. It totally took me by surprise. It blindsided me completely.

"Mr. Crosby, it is you. I saw your name on the patient's list and wondered if it could be you. Remember me? I'm Jamie McQuarters; I used to be in your English class in tenth grade."

"Hi, Jamie. Of course, I remember you. What are you doing here?"

"I'm one of the nurses who assists with the colonoscopies. I'll be in the room with you when the doctor performs your procedure."

"YOU WHAT?"

Oh great. This was not only the worst thing yet, it was the virtual nadir of my teaching career. A former student was going to assist the doctor in looking up my butt. Perfect. I thought of the pharmacy tech at Walgreen's. The outing of the Viagra secret was nothing compared to this.

"Yes, I've been doing this for six years," Jamie said as she wheeled me out of the room.

. . .

All went well with the colonoscopy . . . no polyps . . . no problems . . . if you don't count embarrassment that is. When I awoke and eventually got dressed and left the hospital I didn't see Jamie. In fact, I haven't seen her since.

I wonder if at any of the class reunions she may have attended since that day, she told her classmates, "Remember Mr. Crosby? Well, you won't believe what I saw . . .

"BOB, JUST WHAT ARE YOU TEACHING THESE KIDS?"

In my early days at Northeast, I didn't have my own class-room. Teachers like me were called floaters because we would float from room to room to teach our classes. One of the rooms I shared belonged to my department chairperson, a wonderful lady named Glenda Hill.

Glenda was an excellent department chair. She was very encouraging and supportive especially to teachers like me who were not only young in age but also young in experience at Northeast.

As I would leave Glenda's classroom when my period in it ended, she would be coming into it and in passing she always had a friendly, encouraging word for me. Did I say always? Always except once that is.

It was about March I think, and we were all getting a little antsy waiting for Spring Break. I had taught literature and grammar and vocabulary until I was blue in the face, and I wanted to teach something different–something I knew they hadn't had before. I decided it was the perfect time to teach my memory unit.

Recently I had read *The Memory Book* by former professional basketball player Jerry Lucas and his writing partner Harry Lorraine. I had bought the book a year or so earlier after seeing Harry Lorraine appear on The Tonight Show with Johnny Carson. Harry had dazzled Johnny and his audience with amazing feats of memory. In particular, I remember he recited from memory the names of the people in the first two rows of the theater. Get this. He had met these people for the first time prior to the show as they were standing in line outside. Nothing was written down. He shook hands, got the person's name, and then moved to the next person. Then three hours or more later he came out, and, after talking with Johnny for a few minutes, he recited every name without a miss. Then, he proceeded to tell Johnny that his techniques were all explained in his book–*The Memory Book*.

I went out the next day and bought the book. I loved it. I used it often. Then one day it hit me that I could use it to teach students–not the whole book, but a chapter or two that could help them with their studies. Of course, I always plugged the book, and I'm sure Messers Lorraine and Lucas racked up more than a few sales from my recommendations.

Anyway, on that particular day in Mrs. Hill's classroom, I was teaching the system for memorizing long-digit numbers. Now that's not really an essential thing for most people, but one of the key memory systems of Lorraine and Lucas is the Peg System, and it is based on information that one learns in the memorizing long-digit numbers chapter. So it was important that they learn this or they would be lost in the next section.

Before the students came in for class, I wrote this number 91852719521639092112 on the board. When class began, we reviewed what we had done the day before and talked about a couple of other things before I got to the number on the board.

Without looking at the number I said, "Some of you may have noticed the 20-digit number written on the board. I hope you also have noticed that we are 25 minutes into class and I have not once even glanced at the number."

I said that because kids are famous on test days for running into the classroom and saying, "Hurry up and give the test before I forget," and I wanted them to know that by using the system I was about to teach them, there was no urgency involved. One could remember items learned by using the system for long periods of time without even worrying about forgetting.

So I continued by saying, "Even though I haven't looked at that number for 30 minutes or so now, I'm going to recite it for you using nothing but my memory. And, by the way, after I recite it forward, I will then say it backward too."

With that I began what turned out to be a flawless performance. Every eye was glued to the board. They knew I would miss especially when I started to recite the number in reverse order. But I didn't miss. I played it up big. I made it look as if I were about to stumble but would right myself each time and push on to the end. They were dazzled, and rightfully so I might add. It is no easy feat . . . unless you know the system.

"How did you do that?"

"Tell us what you did!"

"How much time did it take you to learn that?"

These kids were as eager to learn how I had done it as a dog is to have its stomach rubbed. In fact, they almost demanded to know how. For you teachers out there, when is the last time your students demanded that you teach them something? And the sooner the better too! Spring Break was the farthest thing from their minds at that point.

"Okay, if you really want to know, I'll teach you. It's really easy once you learn the chart. One of you asked me how long it took me to learn the number. Would you believe five minutes? It's true. I learned it in no more than five minutes; in fact, it was probably more like two or three minutes," I reported.

"Here's what you need to know first."

Then I told them that each number is represented by a letter and put the list on the board. 1= t or d; 2= n; 3=m; 4=r; 5=l; 6=j or sh or ch; 7=c or k; 8=f or ph or v; 9=p or b and 0=s or z. All other letters have no value whatsoever. So what Lucas and Lorraine do to memorize numbers is to make words using a combination of the letters that represent the numbers and the letters that have no value. They try to form words that create pictures that will be easy to remember. That way a person isn't thinking about the number itself but is working through the image he has created with the words.

The 20-digit number I recited for my class was the one they used in the book as an example. They went through it step by step as I did with my class. First they listed the number.

9 1 8 5 2 7 1 9 5 2 1 6 3 9 0 9 2 1 1 2

Then under it they put the letters from the chart.

B t f l n k d b l n d j m p s p n d d n

Then they filled in with vowels and the other letters that had no value. They formed a sentence with the words. The sentence created an image. That image is what I saw in my mind—not the 20-digit number. I wrote on the board the Lucas and Lorraine sentence.

"*A beautiful naked blonde jumps up and down.*"

I told the class, "While you guys thought I was straining to remember some long as heck number, I was really having the time of my life by remembering what the sentence said and picturing it in my mind. Every time I got to a letter from the chart I would call out the appropriate number. 'Beautiful' is 9185; 'naked' is 271; 'blonde' is 9521; 'jumps' is 6390; 'up' is 9; 'and' is 21 and 'down' is 12. So a beautiful naked blonde is not only an image I'll never forget, but it is also a number I can recite in my sleep."

At that moment the bell rang.

"More tomorrow," I said.

As the students began to file out, about 12 or so stayed behind to ask questions. I had never had a class so interested in anything I had ever taught before. We all had classes to go to so we couldn't stay long, but I tried to answer all of their questions as quickly and efficiently as I could.

Glenda Hill came in to teach her class as I was packing up. She said, "You must have really wowed them today, Bob. They seemed really eager to know whatever it was you were teaching."

"Just a little memory stuff was all it was," I said as I closed my briefcase and headed out the door.

Man, I was proud. Never had I had such success teaching a class before. I even had the attention of the complete deadheads. I must be some teacher I thought without realizing that Jerry Lucas, Harry Lorraine, and their naked blonde example had really done the job. I was just the messenger.

There was something else I didn't realize too. I had forgotten to erase the board. So there, big as life for my department chairperson Glenda Hill and all her English III Honors class to see, was the sentence, "A beautiful naked blonde jumps up and down."

The next day when I came to teach my class, Glenda Hill pulled me aside.

"Bob, just what are you teaching these children? I know you really had their attention yesterday, but I didn't know why until I saw the sentence you left on the board. What in the world was that all about?"

My face turned beet red. How could I have been so stupid?

"I'm sorry, Mrs. Hill. I was teaching them a memory lesson. That sentence wasn't really mine; I got it from the book. I'm not corrupting their morals or anything; I swear." My explanation sounded like about a 9 on the whine-o-meter.

"It's okay," said Glenda Hill. "I knew you weren't doing anything wrong. I just wanted to know so I could tell my class what you were doing. They all want to transfer to your class so they can learn about naked blondes jumping up and down too."

. . .

I continued to teach that unit every year until we moved to block scheduling, but never again did I leave the naked blonde on the board to jump for any other classes but mine.

NO, WE AREN'T DEAD YET!!

My first couple of years at Northeast I wore a nice shirt and tie every day. I'm not sure why. I just did. Now, I'm strictly golf shirts all the way.

This next story happened during my tie-wearing days. It was the first year I had my own classroom.

My room was at the end of the corridor; so to get outside one simply had to exit my room, turn left, go through the corridor exit, and there it was—the great outdoors. Well, actually it wasn't quite the great outdoors. In actuality those maneuvers would take a person out into a tunnel-like corridor which, of course, was open on each end. That so-called tunnel had 3 corridors off it—mine, the middle one, and the far one. Between classes the congestion in the tunnel was sometimes very thick.

The bell had rung to end first period, and students filed out of their classes and headed for second period. But there was something different about this day. Something that didn't usually happen at our school was happening. Coming from the tunnel I could hear chaos—shouting, banging on lockers, cheering . . . you know, chaos. I went outside to see what was happening.

Assembled in the tunnel was a huge throng of students clustered around two girls who happened to be in the process of beating the snot out of each other. I did the logical thing. I stepped in to break it up.

Did I say the logical thing? Let me rephrase that. I did the totally stupid thing. I stepped in to break it up.

There were two choices. I could grab the little bitty girl who weighed about 86 pounds, or I could grab her opponent who was a behemoth that weighed 220 if she weighed an ounce. I chose the 86 pounder. Bad move.

That girl was a bundle of energy. I got around behind her and grabbed her arms. She proceeded to back me into the lockers. My back banged into them. She continued to try to make me turn her loose by banging my backside into the lockers time and time again. She writhed and twisted and turned and squirmed, and it took all I could do to hang on to her. But hang on I did despite her next maneuver which caught me completely off guard.

The little twit began to kick up her heels. She caught me in the shins a couple of times, and it really hurt. I changed my stance. I spread my legs out so when she kicked she would kick air between my legs rather than shinbone. Luckily she was short; had she been taller the spreading of the stance could have been a real bad idea if you know what I mean. I almost started to hope her opponent would come over and belt her one while I held her. It didn't happen and I'm glad it didn't . . . I think.

Eventually, help came in the form of a security guard and a couple of administrators. The girl was subdued, and both she and her adversary were hauled off to the office.

I went back to class where my students pointed out to me my complete state of disarray. Most of my students had seen my feeble attempt at breaking up the fight. More than my inability to control the 86 pounder, they seemed to notice what a mess I was. I hadn't even noticed that my tie was crooked, my shirt pocket was torn, my shirttail was out, there were footprints on my trousers from the knees to the ankles, and I had a big scratch on my face. Of course, my students took great pride in pointing out every flaw to me.

"Mr. Crosby, you're a wreck. Are you all right?"

I looked at myself. Yikes. I was a wreck. Off to the restroom I went to try to make myself presentable again.

When I got back to the classroom, we went about our business as usual. The fight was put on the back burner. I hoped it would eventually fall behind the stove completely and be forgotten. By the end of the period, I had all but forgotten it myself. But I was about to find out in the ensuing periods that my part in the fight was anything but forgotten.

The progression got worse as the day wore on. Someone in third period said, "I heard you got beat up."

A fourth period student said, "What are you doing here? I heard you were in the hospital."

But the clincher came when my last period class showed up and one confused youth said, "Oh good you're here. I heard you were dead, Mr. Crosby."

By the way, it has been at least 29 years since I made that attempt to break up the fight. I learned my lesson, but a thought has crossed my mind from time to time over the years. If I suffered that much damage and humiliation by grabbing the 86-pound girl, what if I had chosen to grab the 220 pounder?

. . .

On a related note, my wife and I went to her 15-year class reunion several years ago. As we were signing in, a classmate of hers named Wally Qualmann was also signing in. This was quite a shock to the people at the desk since old Wally was listed among the classmates who had passed away since graduation.

Several times during the evening, people were overheard saying, "Wally Qualmann? We thought he was dead!"

The highlight of the evening came at the end of the night as they were making presentations to several of the class members. They had awards for things like most children; most times divorced; longest time married, etc. When they came to the prize for the longest distance traveled to get to the reunion, it went to none other than Wally Qualmann. The stated reason?

"He came all the way back from the dead to be here!"

YES, THERE IS A GENERATION GAP

Seldom do I give up any precious lunchtime minutes. Usually
that only happens if there is a newspaper or yearbook deadline that must be met, and we haven't met it yet. Then, yes, I
stuff my face with food as fast as I can and hurry back to my
room to proofread.

This was one of those rare "about to miss the deadline"
occasions. Pages had to go out so I ate in about ten minutes
and went back to my room to edit them. The hallway was
empty except for a lone student who happened to be sitting
on the garbage can located just outside my door. He was not a
student I recognized. He wasn't distinctive in any way other
than he was sitting on the garbage can. There was nothing
ethnic about him. He was just an average teenage Caucasian
boy sitting on a garbage can. Actually, he wasn't just sitting;
he was . . . drumming. No sticks mind you. Just bongoing

away—using the flat part of the plastic garbage can between his legs as the drum.

It looked harmless enough so I didn't say anything to him. Not then, that is.

I went in and sat down at my laptop to begin the page-checking process, but it was no use. The drumming from outside my door was getting on my nerves. I took it for about thirty seconds before I'd had enough. I stormed over to the door.

"Hey, Ringo," I said. "Do you mind?"

He hardly heard me. Evidently he didn't think I was talking to him. So I addressed him again in a little louder tone.

"Yo, Ringo, would you please stop?"

"Stop what?" he asked totally unaware of the problem I was addressing.

"The drumming . . . the pounding . . . the constant beating on the garbage can, that's what. I'm trying to get some work done in here, and it's driving me nuts," I explained in what must have been an exasperated tone.

"Oh, sorry. Sure, I'll stop."

As he climbed down, he said something that threw me.

"I'll stop; but I'm not a gringo."

"Huh?" I said not really knowing if I had heard him correctly.

He repeated himself.

"I'm not a gringo. You called me a gringo when you asked me to stop. I'll stop, but I'm not a gringo."

"No, I said Ringo not gringo. I was calling you Ringo."

"Why were you calling me that?" the befuddled young man asked.

"Ringo . . . you know . . . Ringo Starr of the Beatles. He was their drummer; and you were drumming so I called you Ringo."

"Oh," he said.

I still wasn't sure if he understood me until he said, "My name's not Ringo either."

Then I knew he still didn't get it.

"Okay, you aren't a gringo, and you aren't named Ringo, but you did stop drumming and . . . BINGO . . . that's what counts. Thank you very much."

"Sure, no problem," he said as he wandered off down the hall.

Holy mackerel! I realized once again that there is a huge generation gap out there. I thought everyone had heard of Ringo Starr. Oh, my, my. Guess not.

If I had called him Buddy Rich, I wonder if he would have informed me that he isn't my buddy and his parents aren't rich?

One never knows anymore.

INTERNING?

Many high schools in Broward County, Florida, are what are called magnet schools. This type of school was created initially to help populate some of the schools on the east side of town that are vastly under enrolled each year.

Each magnet school has a theme. For example, one school has the Aviation Magnet; another offers the Emerging Computer Technology Magnet while yet another proffers the Pre-Law and Public Affairs Magnet. Students interested in those particular careers are allowed to go to the appropriate magnet school even though it may be 30 miles from home.

My school has three different magnet academies. We provide the Latin School, the Academy of Architecture and Design, and the Academy of Business and Entrepreneurship.

Our faculty and administration are proud of our magnet students and our academies, but there was one incident that didn't exactly make us proud . . . or did it? Regardless of how we felt about it at the time and how we feel about it now, one thing cannot be denied. It was very definitely in "the spirit of business and entrepreneurship."

This happened several years ago, and there are many versions of the story. In fact, it has become legendary around our school, and its retelling has quite possibly come at the expense of its accuracy. I did not witness it firsthand, but have heard it recounted many times in many different ways from many different sources. This is the version I have most often heard.

It was a Saturday morning and much was going on at school. There was Saturday School, which is both for discipline and for makeup time. There was basketball practice. And there was a craft fair in the main mall of the school.

The craft fair was a fund raiser for the band or the chorus or a club of some sort, and there were many crafts and creations there for public purchase. The craft fair began at 9:00 a.m. Basketball practice began at 10. Saturday School began at 8:00 and was to continue until 11:00.

One of our basketball players (Donald Trotter we'll call him), who, in all candor, was never in jeopardy of being mistaken for our valedictorian, evidently was confused about the time for basketball practice. He showed up just before nine for his ten o'clock practice. With more than a full hour on his hands, he was desperate to find anything to do to kill off the time.

That's when it hit him—a stroke of brilliance. He set out to find the necessary materials he would need. First, he found a partially used piece of poster board. Then, he borrowed a black marker from someone at the craft fair. With those two items he made a sign and headed for the parking lot.

The sign simply read, "Parking, $3.00."

He took his sign and stationed himself at the main gate. As the cars streamed in for the craft fair, he collected three bucks a car.

Meanwhile, in the main mall at the craft fair, one of the parents saw the principal. He asked, "Three bucks is a bit much for parking isn't it?"

"What do you mean?" asked our incredulous principal.

"There's a young man at the gate out there getting three dollars a car from every car that comes into the lot," explained the parent.

Out went the administration. In came Donald Trotter. But what was to be done with him? After all, weren't we the Business and Entrepreneurship Magnet? Wasn't young Master Trotter about as excellent an example of entrepreneurship as our school had seen since we became the Business and Entrepreneurship Magnet? Should we punish him or make him the poster boy for our magnet program?

To this day no one seems to know or to be willing to tell what actually happened to Donald Trotter. Some say they took his money, donated it to the craft fair, and sent him straight to Saturday School. Others say he was scolded publicly but given a pat on the back privately and was allowed to keep the money.

Whatever happened, Donald Trotter's legend lives on. Personally, I like to think of him as our school's first intern in the Academy of Business and Entrepreneurship. Isn't that really what he was?

THE BEST RETIREMENT SPEECH EVER

Every year it seems Northeast High School loses teachers to retirement. Sometimes their partings are tearful, sometimes not. Every retiring teacher is given an opportunity at the last faculty meeting of the year to say a few parting words. Most of the speeches are not really very memorable. Almost never are there any mementos left by the departing ones.

The one exception that I can remember was the year our shop teacher left. His name was Fred, and when old Fred got up to talk, he simply said he wanted to leave Northeast something to remember him by. With that he presented to our principal a handmade toilet paper holder. It was hand carved out of wood and was by far the nicest one I had ever seen. It was to replace the one in the men's restroom in the planning area. That one had been broken for a long time, and Fred, I guess, wanted us to think of him every time we sat down to take care of business. Great gift, Fred. We think of you often . . . at least the male faculty members do.

But Fred isn't really the person this chapter is about. Rather it highlights a gentleman by the name of Al Shuford. Al taught drivers' education, and my first year of teaching was his last year of teaching. I had just survived that first year at Northeast, and we were down to the last day—the one where no students attend but teachers take care of last minute details and then joyfully run to their cars. Turn in grades, go to the luncheon, get our checks, and then head off for 66 days of glorious summer—that was the plan.

Several teachers were ending their careers that day, and one by one each stood to say his/her good-byes. Not only do I not remember what was said by most of them, I don't even remember who they were. But I definitely remember Al.

I had never officially met Al. Ours is a big school with a north and a south campus connected by a large patio area. So it is quite easy to go a whole year or more without ever getting know the teachers on the other campus. In fact, when Al got up to speak, I don't think I had seen him more than two or three times prior to that the whole year.

So what did this elderly, fairly nondescript, retiring gentleman say to make me remember him all these years? Here is his entire speech. I think I can quote him verbatim.

He scared us all at first because he started by saying, "I'd like to share with you the highlights of my teaching career."

"Oh, crap, the highlights of his whole career? This is going to take forever," I remember thinking.

But to my sheer delight and surprise, he uttered just these few words.

"The highlights of my teaching career are . . . *Christmas holidays and summer vacation.*"

Then he sat down.

The applause was thunderous.

PRANKS? NO, THANKS . . . UNLESS . . . THEY'RE REALLY, REALLY FUNNY!

I'm not big on classroom pranks. Usually the kids aren't mature enough to do something fun and let it go at that. So, I make my feelings on the matter known early in the school year, and generally I don't have to worry about that kind of thing happening. There have been, however, a couple of instances of child's play that come to mind that didn't hurt anyone and were very funny at the time.

We've all heard stories of those students who have somehow managed to doze off in class. The standard procedure in a case such as that seems to be not to wake up the kid but to file out quietly when the bell rings and turn out the lights. So when he does finally awake, he will be in a dark room all by himself unable to see a clock or anything else for that matter. That kind of situation is always good for a laugh, but it never happened in my class.

Neither did the instance where the sleeping student was wearing tennis shoes and his shoestrings were tied to the front legs of the desk so when he woke up he couldn't move his legs without first extricating his laces from the chair legs. Ha ha. I never minded hearing about a dozing student getting his just deserts. My feeling was he deserved it because he shouldn't have been sleeping in the first place.

Another incident I heard about but never saw firsthand didn't involve sleeping but did involve one of our math teachers. He had taught for many years, and, in all honesty, really should have hung it up long before this happened to him.

Back in the day, for at least a couple of years there, it seemed we had three or four blackouts a year. The lights would go off. The air conditioning would stop running, and we would be left in total darkness. There was no emergency lighting in the classrooms in those days. There were only two small emergency lights, one at each end of the hallway, and they provided the only light for the entire corridor. The only good to come out of any of the blackouts was it enabled the teachers to determine which kids were the smokers in their classes because as soon as the lights went out, the smokers would take out their lighters and light them.

Many of the corridors in our school are completely inside— with no windows to the outside whatsoever. So when the blackouts occurred, other than those two small emergency lights at the ends of the hallway, there was absolutely no illumination whatsoever (other than the lighters, of course).

Most of the doors to the classrooms have small glass windows, but many teachers cover them to prevent students who are out on bathroom passes or just plain skipping other classes from stopping outside the door and waving to their friends who are in class. (We aren't allowed to cover those windows anymore, but back then almost everyone did.)

In this particular math teacher's classroom, the window in the door was completely covered, and he had no windows connecting to the outside. When the blackouts occurred, he would simply light a candle, and they would wait it out by the light of that lone flickering small flame.

It seems that one time one little prankster in his room got the bright idea of turning off the light switch during the blackouts. That was so when the lights came on in the rest of the school, their room continued in darkness. I guess the theory was, it may not be much fun sitting in the dark, but it beats the heck out of doing work.

Eventually the math teacher was clued in by his fellow teachers who, of course, learned of the prank from students . . . students they had in their classes who were also in the math teacher's class, but couldn't keep their mouths shut regarding all the fun they had had sitting in the dark. As I recall, the clueing in didn't take place until the scene had been repeated on three or four separate occasions.

But these are all pranks that happened to others. What about mine? There is only one, but it was a beauty.

It happened during seventh period. Amazingly I had a wonderful seventh period class. Whenever teachers tell horror stories about their worst classes ever, the stories are usually about a last period of the day class. Evidently I had been living right because my seventh period was the greatest (at least that year it was). It was an SAT Prep class so these were pretty smart kids. We aren't talking about average kids who were struggling to raise their SAT scores to 1000 or so, so they could be accepted into state schools. Rather these were mostly kids who were aiming a lot higher. They wanted 1200's and 1300's that could take them out of state to who knows where. Not only were they a smart class, they were a fun class too.

I love classes that will let me be me . . . you know, those classes where you have very little discipline to worry about. The ones where you can joke around but when it's time to get down to work they understand and actually get down to work. This was one of those. In essence, this class is the kind every teacher dreams of having especially if the teacher has to have a last period class.

On this particular day the class was taking a practice SAT test. They were in the middle of a 30-minute timed section, and I had to go to the bathroom. I didn't want to make a big announcement or anything so I just eased my way to the door and put my hand on the doorknob. All were still working. No one even seemed to notice that I had moved from my desk. I took one last look around, opened the door, closed it quietly behind me, and sprinted down the hall. The restroom was one hallway over so I had to hustle. I burst into the bathroom, did my business, and sprinted back to class. There is no way I was gone for more than three or four minutes.

When I got back to my door, I turned the knob quietly again. I walked in to find my students exactly as I had left them . . . well, almost exactly. They were still sitting quietly taking their test all right, but something was different.

Every desk in the room had been turned around to face the back wall instead of the front. That by itself would have been easy to do, but the hard part was MY DESK HAD BEEN MOVED TOO! It was now in the back of the room rather than the front. It was no light desk either. It must have taken three or four of the beefiest males in the class to move it.

When I walked in and saw what they had done, I fought off my first inclination which was to scold them severely. Instead, I walked to the back of the room (which had become the front of the room), sat down at my desk, and started, as if nothing had happened, to fill out the answer key to the test they were taking.

They began to exchange glances at one another. Has he not even noticed our little prank they must have been wondering? Some began to giggle.

"What?" I asked with as straight a face as I could muster.

"The room . . . don't you notice anything different about it?"

"Sure, I do. Someone erased the board."

They could tell by the twinkle in my eye that I was putting them on so I followed that with this.

"And I noticed that you have rearranged the furniture. Now, I'm noticing one more thing. I am noticing my watch, which will tell me when your minute and a half for putting the room back the way it was is up. Ready . . . go!"

With that I saw firsthand how they had done it. Each student turned his own desk around, and sure enough three hulking lads came instantly to my desk, picked it up with ease, and carried it back where it had been before. A fourth youth requested that I vacate my chair, and then he carried it to the front too. It was all accomplished in under a minute.

Now that's my kind of prank. And it's my kind of class. Why can't they all be like that?

· · ·

Many years later I was talking to my friend Bill Tobias about a former student of ours he had seen somewhere recently.

Bill said, "He's one of the ones who was in that class that pulled that 'turn the desks around' scheme in my room one day when I stepped out for a minute."

"Wait a minute," I said. "What 'turn the desk around' scheme?"

He told me what had happened. His story was identical to mine.

"Who else was in that class?" I asked.

He mentioned several names three of which were names of kids who had also been in that SAT Prep class of mine.

"Great detective work by us," I said. "We just figured out who the instigators were in the room upheaval caper, and *it only took us 20 years to do it!*"

JELLYFISH, KELP, EELS, AND . . . ORANGES?

Bill Tobias was showing slides to his Marine Biology class. It was late in the day, and he had shown the same slides all day long. He was so familiar with the slides that he didn't even have to look at them.

"Now, in this slide you will see a jellyfish. See how it just hangs in the water looking harmless. Don't touch one though or you'll find out just how harmless it isn't."

Click. On to the next slide he went.

"See the kelp here?" he said without looking. "Don't get tangled up in it if you're ever diving near it, or kelp will change to a call for HELP pretty quickly. And, as you may know, it's not easy to yell for help when you are underwater."

Click. On to the next slide he went again.

This procedure continued for several minutes. Click went the remote. Up came the next slide. Out came the description and discussion of it by Bill. It was going very smoothly just as it had every other period of the day.

But then it went wrong. He clicked. The slide changed. He knew what was supposed to be next, and it really wasn't supposed to be funny. Eels are nothing to laugh at he remembered thinking. But his class was in stitches.

He turned around to look. There was no eel on the screen.

Instead, there was a picture of a lady in an orange grove picking an orange off a tree. Her feet were on the ground, but she was stretching up to get an orange off a high limb. It was a Statue of Liberty-like pose but with an orange instead of a torch in her grasp. This scene in itself would not normally have been funny, but when one factors in the fact that the woman was totally naked, it takes on new significance. Especially since it was a full frontal view.

Bill was shocked. It obviously wasn't his slide. Someone had slipped it in among the regular slides unbeknownst to him.

Bill had to laugh right along with the rest of the class.

But how was he to get through the situation?

Quick thinker that he is, Bill simply said, "Now those are some nice . . . um . . . oranges."

Click.

HINDSIGHT CONTINUES TO BE 20-20

Helen Albert, a long-time English teacher at our school, was retiring. She was a wonderful, wonderful teacher and person. Everybody loved her. She had a marvelous sense of humor, and that's probably why I planned to do what I planned to do. Notice I said "planned to do" rather than "did."

There was to be a retirement dinner for her at the local Olive Garden. Generally, I try to contribute something toward the evening's entertainment at these types of affairs. For this particular occasion I had written a poem—a limerick to be more specific. It read:

A teacher from Northeast named Helen
Taught readin' and writin' and spellin'.
She did this for years,
But now all she hears
Is the bell for retirement a knellin'.

Helen was an African-American teacher. She had never been married, but she had some siblings who would be in attendance along with her teacher friends from school. In fact, since it would be mostly people from our school and her family who would be there, I had a little trick up my sleeve that I thought would be good for a laugh. It was designed not only to poke a little fun at Helen but also to make my part seem at least a little longer than just the 15-second reading of that measly five-line limerick I had written.

From the most recessed vaults of my memory bank, I had dredged up a limerick that I had first heard about 35 years earlier—in my middle school days if you can believe that. No, it wasn't from my middle school teaching days; it was from my middle school schooling days. So this one had been rattling around inside me for a very long time.

My plan was to stand up and say, "I wrote this limerick for Helen, and I'd like to read it now."

There once was a lady named Helen
Who came from a place called Dunnelon.
In her efforts to please,
She spread a social disease
From New York to the Straits of Magellan.

Then I was going to act totally shocked and say, "That's not the limerick I wrote. How the heck did that get in there?"

At that point, after the raucous chortling died down, I would read the one that I had written. I would wish her a great retirement, tell her how much her fellow teachers and her students would miss her, and sit down.

There was just one problem. When I arrived, the crowd was not what I expected. Oh, her siblings and her teacher friends were there all right, but about half the audience was made up of members of her church including her minister.

Not knowing any of her church friends, I could just picture myself saying the limerick about Helen spreading a social disease from New York to the Straits of Magellan . . . and absolutely nobody laughing. All through dinner I worried about it.

When dinner was finished, the post dinner festivities began. I was called on to present my poem(s). I stood. I looked around the room. I cleared my throat. I totally chickened out. I could only spit out the limerick about "readin' and writin' and spellin'." I even forgot to tell her how much we would miss her. Totally embarrassed that I had only that silly five-line poem to offer, I turned beet red and sat down. I don't think I was up for even the 15 seconds I thought about earlier. It was more like ten seconds and that was counting throat clearings.

It couldn't have been any worse if I had read the other one and nobody had laughed.

When the evening was over, I went up to Helen and told her my plan and how I had panicked when I saw her minister and the rest of the flock from her church there.

She said, in typical Helen Albert fashion, "Oh, Bob, you should have said them both. They would have loved it. I would have loved it too."

Maybe I was still gun shy from my encounter with the Bacigalupis (see chapter 9). I don't know.

In retrospect I wish I had said both poems there but had not said what I said to the Bacigalupis. But then hindsight is and always will be 20-20.

PINK TENNIS SHOES

A girl on my yearbook staff wore high-top pink Converse tennis shoes to class not too long ago. Boy, did that set me off! Negative memories from days of yore came flooding back to me. This is the kind of negativity I thought only existed with names.

I've talked to several teachers who have said they had to think long and hard about what to name their own children when they were born. It seems that teachers have a definite aversion to giving their own children the same name as any student who has been a problem in class. It's true. I always liked the name Michael . . . until, in my first year of teaching, I had a student named Michael. He was absolutely the student from hell. Just because of him no kid of mine would ever be named Michael.

That's why we named our kids Andy and Lindy. Never had I had a "bad" Andy, and never had I even taught a student named Lindy.

So I knew about the negative effect that names of students could have on teachers, but not until that yearbook student walked in wearing her pink tennis shoes did I realize that student clothing could be just as much a negative as student names.

My wife Mikki and I used to chaperon the Prom just about every year. Mik grew up teaching ballroom dancing for her parents who owned several Arthur Murray Dance Studios. She started teaching at about age 15 and knows everything from the waltz to the tango from the foxtrot to the meringue. I'm no Fred Astaire myself, but she has taught me enough to make me look at least a little like I know what I'm doing out on the floor.

Anyway, when we chaperoned the Prom, we would get out on the floor and dance. Who wants to just go and watch everyone else? And when we danced, we would, well, you know . . . dance. I would lead and she would follow. If a slow song were being played, we would do a foxtrot or possibly a rumba depending on the beat of the music. For faster songs we might do a cha-cha, a swing, or even a three-count disco again based on the beat.

Meanwhile the students would do one of two things. For slow songs they would hang all over each other and barely move except possibly to grope each other; while for the faster ones, they would stand a few feet apart and shake, gyrate, shimmy, or do something completely outlandish that had absolutely no lead and follow to it whatsoever.

The dictionary defines dancing as "moving rhythmically to music" so, in that sense we were all "dancing." But, in all honesty, what Mik and I were doing with the leading and the following that was taking place was much more coordinated than what the kids were doing. With them there was nothing in sync. The girl might be spinning and doing something subtle with her arms while standing six or eight feet from her partner who might be flailing his arms wildly while doing some sort of hop, skip, and jump with his feet. In my mind ours was dancing while theirs was more like . . . well, calisthenics.

At this one particular Prom, we were doing our usual dancing. In fact, we had danced several songs in a row and were in the process of doing a foxtrot when a girl came up to us. We use what is normally recognized as the acceptable dance position—her right hand in my left about shoulder height with my right hand placed just above her waist in the center of her lower back with her left hand resting lightly on my right shoulder somewhere close to my neck. We stand about six inches apart, and there is absolutely no hanging on each other and positively no groping going on as we dance. And that I guess was a problem for this young lady who approached us.

She was not dressed like most of the other girls at this affair. Rather than wearing an evening gown and heels she was attired in a black tuxedo, tails in fact, a pink cummerbund, a pink bow tie, and pink tennis shoes. Yes, pink tennis shoes. She also had a pink flower in her lapel.

She came right up to us and said, "You can't dance like that at the Prom."

"What?" I said not really sure of what she had said but getting ready to be steamed if she had said what I thought she had said.

She repeated it. "You can't dance like that at the Prom."

"What do you mean by that?" I wanted to know although I was pretty sure what she meant.

"I mean you have to get closer and actually dance," she explained.

Actually dance she had said. What did she think we were doing?

"We're the only ones in the place who are actually dancing you little bleep," I should have yelled at her.

I wanted to lead Mik in an underarm turn right about then and catch Miss Pinkie in the chops with a flying elbow, but I restrained myself.

Instead I simply said, "If you can wear pink tennis shoes to the Prom, we can dance any way we want to."

With that I led Mikki in a crosslead box and danced off in a different direction.

. . .

That happened over 20 years ago and I really hadn't given it any thought since then until I saw the girl in the pink tennis shoes in yearbook class that day. Funny how one little thing can set one's teeth on edge. I really thought I was over Miss Pinkie and the irritation she had caused me. Guess not.

LEAVE IT TO BEAVER*

Chris Walsh, formerly an art teacher at Northeast High but prior to that an art teacher at a local elementary school, tells an interesting story about a young lady he had taught when she was in the third grade. It had been six years since those days in the third grade, and the girl had subsequently become enrolled at Northeast as a freshman.

One day she bumped into her former teacher in the hallway. Anyone who might have happened to overhear their conversation must have been confused, embarrassed, convulsed with laughter, or all of the above. According to Chris, the conversation went something like this.

"Hi, Mr. Walsh, remember me?"

"Well, I . . . uh . . . you look awfully familiar . . . are you . . ."

Before he could spit out a name, the girl interjected loudly.

"Come on, Mr. Walsh, you have to remember me, and if not me, *then surely you remember my beaver.*"

Chris Walsh was dumbstruck. Students were passing by in the hall. Many heard what she had said and stopped to hear more. Chris tried to cover himself as best he could.

"Your beaver?" he started.

But before he could finish she said, "Don't tell me you don't remember it. I still remember what you said about my beaver. You said it was definitely the very best one you had ever seen."

Chris Walsh stammered. "I did?"

"Yes, you did. You raved about it. You said you had never seen one so well formed as mine."

This was getting serious. The girl had a companion with her and even she could tell Chris was becoming uneasy with the entire conversation. His agitation was such that he felt he'd better do something immediately to clear himself once and for all.

He said loudly for all the nosey eavesdroppers to hear, "I'm sorry, young lady, but I don't remember your beaver. What's more . . . I know that never in my life have I ever even laid eyes on your beaver much less praised it as much as you say I did."

More students stopped to listen.

"But, Mr. Walsh, you made me think it was so good, I kept it . . . ever since third grade I kept it. In fact, I have it framed and hanging on the wall above my bed."

Chris scratched his head. What the heck was this girl talking about?

Then it all came flooding back to him.

"Oh, your beaver . . . the one you drew in my class in the third grade. Yes, that was outstanding. I do remember it very well now. It really was one of the best I have ever seen. Nice to see you again."

The crowd dispersed, and Chris breathed a big sigh of relief.

. . .

Chris Walsh admitted to me later that he still doesn't remember that girl's name, but he does indeed remember her beaver.

IT WAS JUST A GENTLE LITTLE NUDGE . . . HONEST

It was during another one of those Balderdash sessions. I had explained the rules to the class and had emphasized a couple of things.

"Now, it's very important," I said, "that you write quickly and keep your definitions covered. If anyone sees what you are writing, they'll know it's not the real definition and won't vote for it, and that will cost your team a point. By the same token, please don't come up to my desk while we're playing this game because I'll be writing the real definitions to be mixed in with your fake ones, and if you see what I'm writing . . . well, that won't exactly be fair will it?"

Everyone seemed to agree.

There was a student in the class who was mildly afflicted with cerebral palsy. He was a student I had had in each of the two preceding years in my English classes, but now I had him in SAT Prep. He had very definite physical limitations. In particular, he had a withered left arm, and he dragged a foot when he walked. His mind, however, was as good as any in the class. Except for one thing. He always had to make sure in his own mind that he had everything down pat. He wanted no confusion. Consequently, he would sometimes ask questions the answers to which were fairly obvious.

After explaining the rules to the class and asking if anyone had questions, I looked directly at Barnaby because I knew if anyone had a question, he would be the one. He shook his head. We were set to go.

"Let the fun begin," I said.

I put the first set of words on the board. There were four teams which meant four different words were listed—one for each team. This meant that I had to write very quickly because I had to define each of the four words on small slips of paper. It was while I was in the midst of writing the definitions that the unthinkable happened.

It was quiet—almost eerily so. We were all writing away on our definitions. I was in the middle of defining the fourth word when I looked up. What? I was totally shocked. There, standing right in front of my podium, was Barnaby. Hadn't he heard me say no one could get up and walk around during the game? Evidently he had not because he had quietly walked from his desk near the back of the room all the way up front. Because I had been so engrossed in doing my part in the game, I hadn't heard him or noticed him. The fact that he had walked all the way up to my desk meant that he had walked past at least eight or ten other students who were in the process of writing out their phony definitions, and while standing at my podium, he could easily have looked down to see the correct definitions for the three words I had already defined. In other words, Barnaby was about to screw up the whole game.

I went off.

"Barnaby, what the heck are you doing? Didn't you understand me when I said nobody is allowed to get up and walk around while we are playing this because it will mess up everything? If you had a question, why didn't you ask me before we started the game?"

With that I stepped around from behind my podium.

This next part scared me worse than anything had ever scared me before in school or has ever scared me since in school.

Still talking to Barnaby I said, "You really need to get back to your desk, and don't look at what people are writing as you go back."

I gently placed my hands on his shoulders and turned him around. I pointed him toward his seat and gave him the gentlest of nudges in the right direction.

"Now go," I said.

As lightly as I prodded him nothing should have happened. I guess he was a lot wobblier on his feet than I ever dreamed.

He stumbled. He bumbled. He lurched. He teetered. He tottered. He ricocheted off desks. He careened off students' legs. He pin-balled between rows until finally . . . BAM!!! He went down like he'd been shot.

"OH MY GOD!" I thought. "I've just flattened a kid . . . no, not a kid . . . a handicapped kid! I'm dead!! My career is over. I'll never teach again."

I imagined the headline in the newspaper. EXTRA! EXTRA! TEACHER THROWS AFFLICTED STUDENT TO THE FLOOR . . . OWES FAMILY A TRILLION DOLLARS!

I couldn't get to him fast enough.

"Oh, Barnaby, I'm sorry. Are you all right? Are you hurt? I was just guiding you toward your desk. I didn't mean for you to hit the deck like that. Are you okay?"

Other than my panic-stricken stream of babbling questions, the classroom was quiet. There was genuine concern for Barnaby among his classmates.

"Yeah, I'm okay," said Barnaby slowly.

I picked him up and brushed him off.

"Are you sure? Take a minute here and take inventory. Are you sure you're all right?"

"I'm fine," he said, and he headed back to his seat as if nothing had happened.

I almost wanted to ask him if he would sign a waiver to that effect.

The class looked at me and burst into hysterics. I'm not sure if they were reading my thoughts about the waiver, noticing my ghost-like appearance, or just recalling the ricocheting Barnaby careening off objects, but whatever the cause, they were laughing like crazy. I looked at Barnaby. Even he was laughing. At first I couldn't laugh, but then when I quickly replayed the entire scene in my head, I had to laugh too.

Actually, I was probably laughing because Barnaby was laughing. I might live to play Balderdash in class again after all.

Even now I still don't know why Barnaby came up to my desk that day. For all I know he may have merely wanted to go to the bathroom. All things considered, it's pretty fortunate that I didn't go to the bathroom myself . . . IN MY PANTS!!!

JUST FLUSH HIM!

I have never been the first to arrive at school. In fact, quite often I am among the last to arrive. Not being a "morning person" I like to sleep as long as possible before rolling out to face a new day with new adventures. Teachers are supposed to arrive at my school at 7:15 although first period doesn't actually begin until 7:40. Generally, I would arrive between about 7:32 and 7:40.

To accomplish this 7:32ish arrival time I had to get up about 6:50. Funny thing . . . I know teachers at my school who are already there by 6:50. They have always baffled me. But, anyway, since I don't eat much breakfast, and I shower the night before, it works out just about right if I'm up by 6:50.

At the time this story happened, our children were two and four years of age. Their rooms were on the other side of the house from ours, and they had a bathroom over there as well. Our daughter Lindy had been suffering through a miserable cold, and my wife Mikki had gotten up about daybreak to go over to see how she was doing.

I didn't even know Mik had gotten up when I heard her calling me frantically from the doorway to our bedroom.

"Bob, you've got to get up."

I looked at the clock radio which read 5:55. I still had another 55 minutes before I had to get up.

"No, it's too early," I mumbled as I turned over and pulled the covers up.

"You've got to get up, now," she said firmly. "The kids have a rat in their toilet."

"Well, flush him," I said hoping for any solution that would enable me to stay in bed.

"I did flush him. He won't go," was the reply.

"Flush him again" I grumbled knowing my chances of avoiding personally dealing with this situation were about as good as my chances of being elected President.

"I flushed him three times already, and he's still there so get up and go get him out of there." This wasn't asking; it was telling.

I got up.

"How am I supposed to get him out?" I wanted to know.

"You'll figure it out," she said.

Now that was funny. At my house I'm known as Mr. Badwrench. My wife doesn't think I can fix anything. The reason she thinks that is simple—I can't fix anything. She knows I can't assemble anything either. Heck, according to her I can't even load the dishwasher correctly. In fact, I'm pretty well convinced that she doesn't think I can do much of anything at all correctly. Knowing what a complete boob she thinks

I am at dealing with inanimate objects, I couldn't help but wonder why she thought I was capable of dealing with a real live adversary. Wasn't she even a little worried that I might pull my usual screw-up and somehow let it loose in the house . . . or worse yet somehow let it attach itself to my jugular vein in such a way that only highly trained surgeons could detach it? Or was it just that none of that mattered to her as long as she didn't have to deal with it herself?

I walked into the bathroom and lifted the lid on the toilet. Yep, it was there all right . . . a mouse . . . not a rat. He was just kind of perched there on the porcelain. I flushed him.

Water rushed over him, but he hung on for dear life. I still don't know what he hung on to or how he hung on, but he did. Flushing was definitely not the way to go on this.

But what was plan B? I didn't know, but I did know I wasn't happy. I was standing in the bathroom in my underwear and tee shirt wondering how to outwit a mouse when I should have been enjoying the last 45 minutes or so of my night's sleep.

All of a sudden my attitude brightened. I spied it in the corner almost as if it had appeared as an answer to prayer. The plunger. That's what I would do—I would plunge the little sucker.

I took the plunger in both hands, placed it neatly on top of the mouse, and plunged. Not just once . . . no, this was at least a four-plunge job so I plunged and plunged and plunged and plunged. It was time to look.

I tilted the plunger slightly to one side. He was gone. I had done it. Me—Mr. Badwrench, Mr. Screw Up, Mr. Can't Even Load the Dishwasher Properly—had saved the family from pestilence.

Then something caught my eye—a slight movement coming from the bottom of the plunger. The little rascal had crawled up into the plunger. Hold the victory parade. On to plan C, but what was it?

I thought for a second. Sure, why not? I walked across the bathroom to the door that opened onto the patio. I opened the door and fixed it so it would remain open. The mouse was still inside the plunger so why not lift the plunger quickly out of the toilet and toss it outside? That would work. I just had to make sure I didn't panic and miss the doorway. I could just picture myself being a little off and tossing the plunger into the wall instead of through the open doorway. It would rico-chet off and the mouse would either bounce back and land on that jugular vein I mentioned or would run straight to the kids and eat them. I was determined not to let that happen. I took a couple of slow motion dry runs. I imitated the tossing of the plunger. I worked on my form, my aim, and my follow through. When my confidence was at its highest, I decided to execute the plan. I placed both hands on the end of the plung-er, got a good firm grip, and in one fluid, athletic movement lifted it, turned, and tossed it directly though the doorway.

It was a beautiful toss . . . a world-class toss. The plunger turned end over end, went through the doorway, and bounced on the patio outside. When it hit the ground the first time, it bounded high into the air and expelled its passenger . . . into the pool.

Well, so much for that little intruder I thought as I fetched the plunger, put it away, and headed back to bed.

I passed Mik in the living room.

"Did you get him? she asked.

"Yep, sure did," I boasted barely resisting the urge to put my thumbs in my armpits and strut.

"Good going; where is he?"

"He's in the pool," I explained.

"HE WHAT? YOU CAN'T LEAVE HIM IN THE POOL!! She was practically screaming at me.

I wanted to ask why not, but knew better.

Out to the pool I went.

He wasn't hard to find once I got out there. He was swimming around seemingly having the time of his life when an idea hit me.

Our pool is screened in, but we do not have screen over the top because it blocks too much sunlight. We get much more use out of the pool by not having screen on the top. Now I was even happier about our decision to leave the top screenless because I could see how this could be a big benefit in helping me get the mouse out of the pool.

I didn't just want to get him out only to have him escape onto the patio. If that happened, it would certainly be just a matter of time before he somehow made his way back into the house. No, I had to get him out into the yard . . . better yet I had to get him out into the neighbor's yard.

I picked up the skimmer. As he swam by, I would scoop him up and toss him high into the air. If all went as I imagined it, he would not only clear our screened in area but would also clear the fence that separated our yard from our neighbor's yard. Maybe he would land in their pool or at least on their grass. I didn't want to kill him; I just didn't want him bothering us again.

I tried to scoop him two, three, four, five times. Every time he scurried off the skimmer and swam away.

The clock was ticking. It was 6:35. Going back to bed was quickly becoming a non-option. That was irritating me.

The cold was irritating me too. I was standing barefooted, still clad only in my underwear and tee shirt in about 55-degree weather. Every time the rodent escaped the skimmer I got colder and colder and madder and madder.

I'm not proud of what I did next, but, in retrospect, I think it had to be done. I saw a broom leaning up against the wall. I grabbed it, and the next time the little bleep swam past I put it on the back of his neck. I held him under water. He tried to escape, but he was caught fast in the bristles of the broom. Little bubbles rose to the surface of the pool. They continued for a short time and then the struggling stopped. The mouse was dead. I turned the broom sideways, scooped him up on the flat surface, and carried him to the outdoor garbage can.

When I went back inside, I went straight to bed. As I got in and pulled the covers up two things happened. First, Mik came in.

"He's dead," I said before she even had a chance to ask.

"Where is he?" she wanted to know.

"I put him in the garbage can out front."

"Did you put him in a plastic bag and tie it up?"

"No, and I'm not going to," I said. "I'm going back to sleep."

Then the second thing happened.

The alarm sounded and I had to get up.

. . .

When I got to school that day, I decided to share my adventure with my classes. The kids all gave me a hard time about killing the little critter. Drowning it was not a very humane thing to do in their eyes I guess.

In one class after I had finished telling my story, a girl raised her hand. It was a girl whose father was also a teacher at our school.

She said, "That happened to us too. My dad was at a meeting one night, and I went into the bathroom to take a shower and saw a giant rat in the toilet. I ran out and told my mom. We went back in, put the toilet lid down, blocked the bottom of the doorway with towels and waited for my dad to come home."

"Well, what happened?" I asked.

"When he got home, he went into the bathroom and lifted the toilet lid, but the rat was gone. He looked around the bathroom and spotted the rat on top of the shower rod. Then he shut the door and went to the closet in the hallway."

Yikes! This was better than my story.

"What did he do then?"

"He got out his bow and arrow, went back into the bathroom and shot an arrow right through the rat."

That class didn't think I quite so inhumane as the others.

. . .

The next day my other classes had to admit that how I had handled my situation wasn't so bad after all. Two things changed their minds. I told them the Robin Hood-like skewering of the rat by that girl's father and I also told them what I had learned at lunch the day before.

When I told the story to my fellow teachers in the lunchroom, my friend Chip Shealy said a similar instance had happened to him. He said his neighbor had come over to his house one day to ask him for some assistance. Her husband was out of town, and she had a rat in her toilet and didn't know how to deal with it. Chip went over and sized up the situation. What he did made me look like I should be nominated for the

Humanitarian of the Year Award after the way I tried first to save my adversary before killing him.

What Chip did was go to the kitchen where he found an empty coffee can and a butcher knife. He went back to the bathroom and put the can over the rat's body. Then he quickly brought the blade of the knife down on its neck.

Ouch!!!

No wonder I improved in their eyes.

THE ESSENCE OF AP ENGLISH*

Dr. Sandra Melillo (Sandy to her friends) is a 4-foot 10-inch bundle of energy who does everything at our school. She is the department chairperson for the Language Arts Department; she directs all the faculty plays; she runs NETV which airs the morning announcements on closed circuit television; she teaches the Advanced Placement senior English class (affectionately known as AP); she is currently writing a musical; she . . . well, you get the picture. I get tired just thinking about all the stuff she does.

Even the greatest of the great have their moments, however, and one of hers came not too long ago when she was teaching the philosophies of Aristotle and Plato to her AP class.

"A thing has an essence about it that distinguishes it from all other things. A dog has dogness. A tree has treeness," she instructed.

It seemed like a simple concept to understand.

She continued, "Aristotle believed that since dogness can be found in all dogs, that essence of dog can be called a 'universal.' Universals do not exist apart from actual things in the world. In contrast, Plato believed the essence of things is called a 'forum' and these forums exist in another world. In using the concept of dogness, Plato believed that individual dogs—Butch, Spot, Fido, and Snoopy, etc.—participate in that forum of dogness and are called dogs because of that participation."

Now, AP classes, as a rule, are comprised of the sharpest kids in the school. But just because they are sharp doesn't automatically make them good AP students. The good Dr. Melillo thought it would be the perfect time to juxtapose the beliefs of Plato and Aristotle with the beliefs of Melillo. She wanted to convey the thought that all AP students should have that AP essence about them. Just being smart is not enough. There is so much more that is needed to be a true AP student.

It was in trying to communicate that thought to her students that she said, "So it is indeed my sincere hope that all of you will soon achieve AP-ness."

The class was in shock. Did they actually hear her correctly?

"You want us to achieve what?" one of the students asked.

"AP-ness, AP-ness . . . you all need to achieve AP-ness. Dogs have dogness; trees have treeness; AP students must achieve AP-ness . . . and the sooner the better," she said firmly.

"Doc . . . do you know what you're asking?" asked one of the girls.

"Certainly, I do. AP-n . . . OH MY GOD!" She stopped in mid-sentence. She finally heard in her own voice what the students had picked up on the first time she said it.

"You know what I mean . . . not a penis . . . but AP-ness . . . you know, the essence of AP," she tried to explain but by then the class was up for grabs.

Then she bared her soul.

"That's what always happens to me. I was trying to sound so erudite. It never fails. When I do that, I always end up right back down in the gutter. Funny how when I arrive there, some of my students are always there before me."

· · ·

Sandy had a similar incident happen a few years prior to that. When Clarence Thomas was nominated for the Supreme Court, he was accused of sexual harassment. One of Sandy's students had watched some of the hearings regarding the matter on television, and he was confused about something.

"Mrs. Melillo, sometimes they say harass (and he pronounced it like the name Harris), and sometimes they say harass (and he pronounced it like the words 'her ass'). Which is it?"

Sandy grabbed a dictionary. As she turned quickly through the pages she announced to the group, "Okay, I'm looking up harass." Because she herself always uses the second of the aforementioned pronunciations, it sounded as if she had said, "Okay, I'm looking up her ass."

Unlike with her AP-ness faux pas, she got this one right away and burst into laughter as soon as she said it.

SCHOOL . . . WHERE CONVERSING
CAN BE A PLEASURE

Tom Popovics is one of the best-liked teachers at our school. Students enjoy his classes for many reasons, but one of the main reasons is he talks to them as people. During down time he converses with them—sometimes individually, sometimes as a group—about anything and everything.

Tom told us at lunch one day that not too long ago, he was walking up and down the aisles of his classroom while his students were doing a worksheet. As he passed by this one desk, he saw a pen lying on the floor next to the desk. When he picked it up, he read the words printed on it. "Publix—Where Shopping is a Pleasure" it read.

"Publix is a good store," he said to the pen's owner just trying to make small talk.

The girl made a face and said quite unenthusiastically, "Yeah, I guess so."

"Do you work there?" Tom asked.

"Yeah, I work there. My whole family works there. My dad is manager of a Publix. My mom is an assistant manager of a different Publix, and I work there too."

"If you don't mind my saying so, you seem to have a pretty negative attitude about a store that feeds your whole family," Tom observed.

"Well, it's not the store exactly . . . it's the people."

Tom wanted a clarification. "The people who work there?"

"No," answered the student, "the people who shop there—they're weird."

"Wait a minute," Tom said. "I shop there."

"I don't mean everyone who shops there. I mean . . . well . . . at my mom's store there's this homeless woman who comes in two or three times a week."

"She's homeless, but she comes in to shop?" Tom asked.

"No, not to shop."

"What for then?"

"She comes in to clean the bathrooms."

"Oh, she works there," Tom clarified.

"No, she doesn't. She just comes in and cleans the bathrooms."

"Just for the fun of it?" Tom wanted to know.

"I guess so," answered the girl.

"And they let her just clean the bathrooms for no pay?"

"She does a good job."

"But shouldn't they pay her something if she does such a good job?"

"Well, they sort of pay her," the girl offered.

This was like pulling teeth.

Tom tried to get to the nub of it. "How do they sort of pay her? Usually people either get paid or they don't."

"My mom pays her."

"Out of her own pocket?"

"No."

"How then?"

"She gives her chicken and cigarettes from the store."

Tom laughed out loud.

"Why chicken and cigarettes?" he asked.

"That's all she wants," said the girl. "I told you the people are weird."

Tom had to admit they were . . . at least that one was any way.

And to think he would have missed out on this entire Publix saga had he not commented on her pen.

. . .

When Tom teaches his freshman world history class and gets to the section on the Greeks, he has a unique way of getting his class to remember what the Greeks are known for in history.

He tells them, "When you're thinking about the Greeks, just remember they are famous for three things, and they all start with the letter D. The 3 D's of Greek civilization are . . . Drama, Democracy, and Da Olympics."

. . .

No chapter on Tom Popovics and/or the Greeks would be complete without mentioning his standing joke regarding the big vase-like object that sits on the end table in our teacher's lounge. When newcomers infiltrate us, he will sometimes ask as he points to the vase, "Do you know what that thing is?"

Usually they don't know or won't offer an answer so he tells them, "It's a Grecian Urn."

Then a fellow teacher who is in cahoots with Tom will chime in with, "Oh, really? What's a Grecian urn?"

Every time Tom answers, "About $5.50 an hour."

And every time we laugh.

Why?

We don't know, but we do.

REMOTE POSSIBILITIES

Kckcckkkkkkkckckckckckkkkkkkkkkckcckkckckckcckkckc!
That, my friends, for lack of a better way to indicate it, is my
version of the spelling of static. Static? Yep, that sound that
accompanies the snow on a television screen when there is no
picture but there is a totally obnoxious and annoying sound.
To me it just sounds like kckcckkkkkkckckckckckkkkkkkkk-
kckcckkckckckcckkckc.

My son Andy tells the story of a bit of high jinks that went
on at his school when he was a freshman. A friend of his had
a universal remote that he took to school and programmed
to work the classroom televisions. There were a couple of incidents which I'm glad didn't happen to me although if some
kid had tried to pull these on me, I hope I would have been
at least a little suspicious that I was being had—more than
these two poor unsuspecting teachers were anyway.

The first of the two incidents happened in a last period of the day social studies class. It is important to understand the configuration of the classroom as classroom set up plays an important role in the carrying out of the plan. Two doors, both of which were on the back wall, opened into the classroom, and the way the desks were arranged made it a much wider classroom than it was long. Traditionally, a class will have five or six rows of desks with five or six desks per row. This particular room had about nine rows with only four desks per row. The teacher's desk was in the front left corner of the room, and the television/VCR combination was on a stand in the front right corner. It was situated in such a way that the teacher could not see the television screen from his desk.

The television was basically just for showing video tapes. Now, if no tape were in the machine but the television was on and tuned to channel three, a blue screen would show. There would be no sound accompanying the blue screen; however, if tuned to any other channel, a screen of the dreaded television snow would appear and with it would be the repulsively annoying almost nerve-fraying kckcckkkkkkckckckckckkkkkk sound (if the sound on the set were turned up that is.) Thus the ingredients of the totally quiet blue screen contrasted with totally obnoxious static screen and a universal remote in the hands of a playful freshman made for ideal circumstances for chicanery.

Universal remote boy, or UR boy as we will henceforth refer to him, took advantage of a couple of things that happen routinely at the end of every school day to execute his carefully concocted scheme. A minute or two before a high school class ends, especially at the end of the day, kids get a little antsy and a little noisy. Also, the teacher in this particular class never got out of his desk chair as school was about to end for the day. He would always continue to sit at his desk and pack up his things even as the bell rang and the students filed out. So as the end of the day tumult began on this particular day, UR boy swung into action.

"Psst, Andy, watch this," UR boy said to my son as he got out his remote and turned on the television from his seat.

"What are you doing?" Andy wanted to know.

"Just watch; but while you're watching, pass the word along that no one is to say anything about the TV being on."

Word spread throughout the classroom. Some of the students hadn't even noticed that the set had been turned on, and the teacher, because of the angle of his desk, certainly didn't notice either. Those who had noticed said nothing.

UR boy whispered, "I'm going to set this up so we can have some fun after the bell rings."

"Why not now?" Andy inquired.

"You'll see," was the reply.

With that he hit the mute button on the remote, and at the same time he turned the volume up as loud as it would go. Because the television was set on channel three, no sound could be heard anyway, but by hitting the mute button, it allowed UR boy to change to any other channel without hearing the static sound that was always on those other channels.

When the bell rang, the class filed out. UR boy left by one door, but once out in the hallway he turned and walked quickly toward the other door that led into the classroom. As he passed that other door, the one directly in line with the television, he unmuted the sound.

KCKCCKKKKKKCKCKCKCKKKKKKKKKC!!!!!

"OHHHHHHHH!" shouted the teacher as he all but jumped out of his skin. He must have felt as if he were being attacked by aliens or terrorists as the obnoxious sound filled his classroom.

The noise was unbearable, but he didn't know where to go first. Should he run to the set and turn it off; or should he run out into the hallway to see if a clue could be found as to what had happened?

He opted to turn down the set.

The next day the entire scene repeated itself. Evidently the teacher must have felt that no one would dare do that to him again; either that or he had completely forgotten the incident from the day before. Either way, he was not prepared for the recurrence that happened on day two.

It was almost a carbon copy of the previous day. The only difference was this time the teacher moved quickly to the hallway to see if he could catch anyone looking suspicious. He couldn't.

On the third day the fun ended. UR boy was never caught, but when he came into class on day three he immediately noticed something was different . . . the television set had been unplugged.

. . .

Such joy was had with the muting and the unmuting that other "remote possibilities" had to be contrived. In English class another opportunity presented itself.

The class was watching a video of the movie version of a book they had just finished reading. As they sat staring at the screen, UR boy struck again. Because the set had no volume bar to register the raising or lowering of the sound, it could be turned up or down with the universal remote, and no one could see that it was being done. Only the sudden inability to hear what was being said let everyone know that something was going awry.

"Miss Gross, we can't hear it," one student said.

Miss Gross got up, went to the set, and turned up the volume. Once she had turned it back to a normal level she headed back to her desk, but UR boy acted again. This time, however, he made the volume go louder and louder. By the time she sat down, the set was blaring full blast.

"Miss Gross, you turned it up way too much," someone said.

She got up and went back over to the set. As she approached it, the sound leveled off again. It was back to normal.

She stopped and headed back to her desk. Oddly, as she turned, the sound dipped, and the voices became almost inaudible. She turned back to the set. The sound leveled again.

She went to the set. She stopped the tape. She turned off the television. She waited thirty seconds. She turned it on again. She adjusted the sound.

"There. Can everyone hear it?"

She stood there for a minute or more. Everything was fine. The sound was steady.

Miss Gross headed back to her desk once again, but the second she took her first step the sound dipped again. She stopped in her tracks. She turned back toward the television, moved to it, and placed her hand on it. Miraculously, the sound came back to normal.

She tried it again. As she turned around again, the sound dipped again. When she returned and touched it again, it seemed to right itself again.

"This is the strangest thing I have ever seen in my entire life," she said to the class.

"Miss Gross, there must be something inside you that is causing the sound to go crazy," UR boy said with the slight trace of a grin on his face.

Miss Gross never suspected that someone was toying with her sanity.

"Well, I guess I'll just have to stay right here then," she reasoned.

And she did. She stood by the television for the rest of the period as her class watched the movie.

. . .

The next day when UR boy's class arrived, and they were about to begin watching the rest of the movie, Miss Gross was quite excited.

"I don't know what I did to fix the television set," she said, "but whatever it was, it worked in all my other classes. The sound was fine for all of them. It must have just been a loose wire or something that fixed itself when I put my hand on the television."

She turned on the set and started the tape.

UR boy didn't have the heart to torment her any further.

IT'S THE SHORT, WHITE WOMAN'S TURN

Every year each school selects one teacher as its teacher of the year. It is quite an honor to be selected.

When I had my turn back in the 1996-1997 school year, I was thrilled . . . at first. Then when I saw how much work was involved in writing essays and filling out paperwork and all the other gobbledygook that goes along with the honor, I wished I had never even been nominated much less been selected to represent our school.

The reason for all the essays, etc., is that a teacher of the year for the entire county is selected from the winning teachers of all the different individual schools, and it is from those essays and that paperwork that finalists are chosen for interviews.

I was not selected as a finalist. But I did get to go to the luncheon where the county's teacher of the year was named. So I knew firsthand what the entire process was like.

In the 2006-2007 school year the teacher of the year from our school was the magnificent Dr. Sandy Melillo. Sandy is a 4 foot 10 inch 87-pound bundle of energy who is loved by all who know her. Her students adore her; her fellow teachers respect her and trust her as the voice of reason; and the administration knows it can count on her for anything and everything. So to say we were all pulling for her to win the county teacher of the year award on the day of the big luncheon is perhaps the understatement of the century.

As our own lunch period ended around one o'clock somebody said, "Well, I guess Sandy didn't win or we would have heard something by now." I remember thinking at that time that the announcement of the winner didn't happen until around two o'clock the time I went to the luncheon so I still held out some hope.

Around 2:15 the announcement came. The intercom came on and the mellifluous yet excited voice of Liz Tatum, one of our assistant principals, proudly announced the great news. "Dr. Sandy Melillo has just been named Teacher of the Year for Broward County."

Not all of the 2,000+ students in our school know Dr. Melillo but those who do know her as well as all the teachers couldn't help but be thrilled. I remember smiling from ear to ear and actually clapping as I heard the news while sitting at my computer during my planning period. I heard others clapping and shouting in other classrooms too.

We all knew that if ever there were a truly-deserving teacher for that honor it was Sandy. However, I guess maybe everyone doesn't have the same criteria for teacher of the year.

Jim Selbach, a math teacher at our school and a good friend of mine, told me what happened in his classroom when the announcement was made.

"The announcement came on that Sandy had won, and I immediately starting clapping," explained Jim.

"Then one of my students asked me why I was clapping."

I said, "One of our teachers is teacher of the year for the entire county. And besides that she's a friend of mine. That's why I'm clapping. Don't you think that's a pretty big deal?"

The kid thought for a second and then asked a seemingly unrelated question.

"Did you read the article in the paper a couple of weeks ago about the teacher who was having sex with some of the boys in her class?"

"As a matter of fact, I did," responded Jim. "So what?"

The kid remarked without hesitation, "Well, to me . . . *she's the teacher of the year!!!*"

Jim could only shake his head.

. . .

A week after it was announced that Sandy had won, we had a celebration for her after school. We had hamburgers and hot dogs and a big cake congratulating her.

Sandy's husband Rick was there, and I asked him what his first thought was the week before when they announced her name as the winner.

"Wow" was all he could say at first. Then after a second he said, "It's a matter of being in the right place at the right time. I mean there are so many deserving teachers; I think they just vary it from year to year. One year an African-American elementary school teacher will win and then you won't have another teacher in that category win again for a while. The next year it will be a male middle school phys. ed. teacher's turn to win. I guess this year it must have been the short, white, high school teacher's turn."

I didn't tell Sandy what he said . . . until now that is.

Don't make him sleep on the couch, Sandy. He's really extremely proud of you, just like we all are!!

TWO NICKS EQUAL ONE PONCHO

It's usually an annoyance when teachers have two students with the same first name in a class. Here is a typical scene.

"Okay, who can conjugate the verb 'to run' for me? How about you, Nick?"

No answer.

I pause.

I stare at him. Still nothing.

Even though I'm staring directly at the Nick I've called on, there is still no answer. There is no eye contact either. He knows I'm calling on him, but he doesn't answer. And the reason he doesn't answer is obvious. He knows about as much about conjugating verbs as a cocker spaniel. But he can't just say, "I don't know, Mr. Crosby." No, he has to play this other game. And he plays it because he has an ace in the hole. That ace? It's the other Nick.

So I repeat the question and call on Nick again, but this time I use a last name as well. "Nick Harper, can you conjugate the verb 'to run' for me?"

"Oh, did you mean me, Mr. Crosby. I thought you meant the other Nick."

I always wanted to say, "No you didn't, you little creep. You knew I meant you, but you didn't answer NOT because you didn't think I was talking to you but because you not only don't know how to conjugate the verb "to run" you don't know anything, nada, zip, zero," but I never did.

Anyway, one day I decided I had had enough of this silly little game. It started just about as I described it above but almost immediately took a bit of a turn .

I asked a question and called on Nick. Nick, the cocker spaniel equivalent, didn't answer, but this time the other Nick spoke up.

"Mr. Crosby, would you mind calling one of us Nick and the other one Nicholas because every time you say Nick I really don't know if you are talking to him or me."

"Now, that's a reasonable request," I said, "but I think I'll get confused calling one of you Nick and the other Nicholas. I won't remember who's who, but I think I do have a solution based on actual personal experience of my own."

Oddly enough this really did happen to me when I was in the tenth grade, and it was ironic that I was about to apply my tenth grade experience to the tenth grade class I was teaching.

I continued, "Back when I was in the tenth grade, I had a Spanish class. The teacher called us by our Spanish names. Because my name is Robert, the teacher called me Roberto. Well, not really. She really called me Roberto Uno because there were two Robertos in the class. I was Roberto Uno, and the other kid was affectionately known as Roberto Dos. She tried to make that work for a couple of weeks before she gave it up."

"Senorita Bland said, 'I can't keep you two straight. One of you needs to change your name. Roberto Uno, I think from now on I'll call you Ricardo.'"

"Fine. I became Ricardo," I told the class. The two Nicks seemed to be wondering where this was heading.

"But guess what? About a week later a kid from another of her classes transferred into our class. His name—yep, you guessed it—he was called Ricardo. For a week or so she tried the Ricardo Uno for him and Ricardo Dos for me thing, but that was confusing for her. Heck, it was even confusing for me because whereas I had been Roberto Uno before, now I was Ricardo Dos. Caramba!

"This time she left the choice up to me," I continued telling the class.

"She said, 'Ricardo Dos because you have already changed once it might as well be you who changes again. Why don't you pick a name and you can go by that from now on. What would you like to be called?'"

My English class was really into this story. Every eye was on me. Every kid seemed interested in how I was going to solve the case of the two Nicks.

I went on, "Now, the kid who sat behind me in the class was a bit of an instigator. He was whispering to me. 'Say Pierre; I dare you. You got no guts at all if you don't say Pierre.'"

I could tell by the smiles on their faces that most of my English students were sharp enough to know that Pierre is a French name and since I was in Spanish class, Pierre would hardly have been suitable.

"Now what I haven't told you guys is my Spanish teacher scared the bejeebers out of me on a daily basis. She was a good teacher, but she absolutely put up with no crapola. So, on the one hand, I wanted to prove I had guts by saying I wanted my new name to be Pierre, but, on the other hand, I knew she would not find it amusing if I did. Everybody else would love it, but she would have despised it and me too. So at the last possible instant, sanity prevailed. I had already begun to form the word Pierre when I detoured.

"Pi . . . oncho. I mean Poncho, Senorita Bland. I want to be called Poncho."

And Poncho it was. And not just for the remainder of that year. No. I was lucky enough to have Senorita Bland in my junior and senior years too. So I got to be called Poncho for three solid years!

"Now, class, you're probably wondering why I told you that story. Well, here's why. From this day forth, Nick Harper, you are Poncho."

It felt good. Even though it was the other Nick who had asked for the change, I was zapping Nick Harper with the Poncho epithet. After all, he was the irritating one—the one who always pretended not to think I was calling on him. He deserved to be Poncho.

As it turned out, however, the joke was on me. He loved it. He started signing his papers as Poncho. In big letters on his notebook he wrote, "THIS NOTEBOOK BELONGS TO PONCHO!"

Looks like I misjudged him. He was really more like a chihuahua than a cocker spaniel.

SOME KIDS ARE JUST FUN TO MESS WITH

Any teachers who may be reading this will admit, I'm sure, that some kids are just fun to be around. It's so much fun to mess with those types. I'll even go so far as to say that it's those who are fun to mess with but who also know when it's time to quit messin' around and get down to business who are generally our favorites.

Chip Shealy tells the story of a boy—one of those fun to mess with types—who in class one day asked to go to the restroom. The exchange went something like this:

"Mr. Shealy, may I go to the restroom?"

"Sure, Isaac, if you'll go for me while you're out there."

"What do you mean?" asked an incredulous Isaac.

"I mean I have to go too, but I can't leave the classroom so while you're out there going for you will you go for me too?"

"How am I going to do that?" Isaac wondered aloud.

"That's for you to figure out," said Shealy with a twinkle in his eye.

"Okay," said a perplexed Isaac who seemed to have absolutely no idea he was being had.

He was about to leave when Shealy stopped him again.

"Wait a minute, Isaac. How are you going to go for me if you don't know what I have to do?"

"Huh?"

"You don't know if I have to go peepee or pooh-pooh," said Shealy with a straight face.

"Well, which is it? asked Isaac.

"Peepee," said Shealy.

Out went a bewildered Isaac to the absolute glee of his classmates.

A short time later Isaac returned.

"Well, do you feel better? asked Chip.

"Yes."

"Did you go for me?"

"I guess so," said Isaac.

"I thought you did because I feel better too. Thanks."

Isaac sat down wondering if he should be proud that he was in some way able to help out his teacher or if his teacher was in dire need of some sort of psychiatric treatment.

· · ·

It's incidents such as that one with Isaac that not only keep teachers sane and able to ward off boredom but also help make teaching fun. The key to it all, however, is making sure you use the right kid for the humor. It has to be a gullible type, one the other students in the room like so they won't make fun of them for the rest of the year, and one who won't get his or her feelings hurt by the "game."

I had one such type in my college review composition class several years ago. Her name was Kelly, and she was one of the sweetest most likable girls I had taught in a long time. She was loved by her classmates for her personality but maybe even more for her naïveté. She was the perfect "pigeon" I guess you could say, and I wanted to take advantage of that fact in much the same way that Mr. Shealy had toyed with Isaac. She was such an easy mark or so I thought.

So one day, without having planned it out beforehand, I did something to "mess with" Kelly. It was totally spontaneous and that is part of what made it fun. I'm not sure that if I had thought it out ahead of time, I would ever have done it. I probably would have talked myself out of it altogether. But since it was so spontaneous, I couldn't seem to resist doing it.

We were about to embark upon a lesson in paragraph development, and I was passing out the skeletal outline that we would be using during the period. When I teach and expect the class to take notes, I like to split the difference with them. Usually, I do this by giving them a partial outline, and as we discuss things, they are expected to fill in the missing parts. The skeletal outline for the lesson on paragraph development looked like this.

Methods of Paragraph Development
A.
   1-
   2-
B.
C.

1-

2-

D.

Most people could glance at the outline and immediately tell by the presence of the letters A, B, C, and D that there were four methods of paragraph development that we would be discussing.

When I pass out outlines and such to the class, I never do it the way most teachers do and give the first person in the row the number needed for the students in the row. Instead, I walk around and hand each kid one. It takes a minute longer, but it works out much better especially since when doing it the other way I always seemed to give the first person in the row the wrong number and then all sorts of commotion would follow when a row had too many or came up short.

Well, Miss Gullible, sat in the last seat in the last row and it was as I approached her seat to give her the outline that the idea struck me. She had proven during the time I had had her as a student that she would believe anything and everything anyone told her. As we all know, that can sometimes be a dangerous proposition in life so I thought I should take it upon myself to show her firsthand why she should be cautious about what she accepts and doesn't accept as the gospel truth.

As I handed her the outline, I whispered a question about it.

"Kelly, how many methods of paragraph development do you think there are?"

Kelly looked at the sheet.

Then she answered me with a question of her own, "Are there four?"

"Yes, it looks like it doesn't it. But what if I told you there are really five? When I get back to the front of the class, I'm going to say, 'Well, class, how many methods of paragraph development do you think there are?' They'll all say four, but you raise your hand and when I call on you, you say there are five. Everyone will wonder how you know something they don't know. You'll look really smart."

"Okay, that'll be cool," she said never wondering for a second why I would allow her the honor of correcting the others or why I would pass out an outline that was wrong!

Had she thought just for a second she could have figured me out, but she didn't.

When I arrived back up front I said, "Well, class, today we'll be discussing the methods of paragraph development. How many methods of paragraph development do you think there are?"

Just about everyone responded with, "Four."

A hand in the back of the room went up. Kelly was right on cue. I called on her.

"Yes, Kelly?"

"Mr. Crosby, there really five methods of paragraph development."

Then came the shocker for old Kell.

"No, Kelly, I'm afraid not. There are only four just as the outline indicates."

"But you said for me to say there are five."

"I know, but there are really only four which proves what?" I asked.

"I guess it proves I shouldn't believe everything I hear," said Kelly.

"Bingo. That's exactly what it proves."

The class laughed at Kelly's continued gullibility, but then she said something that caught everyone, especially me, off guard.

"But, Mr. Crosby, it proves something else too."

"Oh, yeah, what else does it prove?"

"It proves you're a big, fat liar."

You know; she had me there.

THAT'S THE MASCOT OF COLUMBIA UNIVERSITY?

For years I taught the verbal portion of the SAT to juniors and seniors. The way it worked was I would teach the verbal portion of the test to a class of about 25 students while a math teacher would teach the math portion to a different 25 or so. At the end of the nine weeks, we would switch classes, and I would then teach the verbal part to the ones who started with math, and the math teacher would teach the math part to the ones who started with me.

At least that's the way it usually worked. One year for some reason we only had 30 students sign up for the course. Actually, it was a good thing we had so few because the math teacher who always taught the math part left at the end of the first semester and we had no one else to teach the math part. So the plan was for me to keep all 30 students for 18 weeks instead of nine. Not being a math teacher myself there was no way I could teach the math, so I had to come up with college-related things to teach for the additional nine weeks.

I taught speed reading, my memory unit, and a bunch of other stuff but at the rate I was going it looked as if I might run out of things to teach about three weeks early.

Panic does some amazing things at times, and this was no exception. I decided to have my students research colleges and make PowerPoint presentations to the rest of the class. I allowed two or three students to work together. They had to have at least a 12-slide presentation showing pictures of the campus and giving pertinent information such as tuition costs, academic programs offered, athletic teams, fraternity and sorority information, and anything else they felt was noteworthy about the college.

This was a stroke of brilliance on my part. They really got into the research and the making of the PowerPoint presentations. It took several days to prepare it all, and then it took a couple more days to show the completed presentations to the class. All in all, it was a wonderful idea because of the educational opportunity it afforded them, and, more importantly, because of how much time it ate up so I didn't have to come up with anything else to get me to the end of the year.

For me it was wonderful for another reason. It provided maybe the most memorable answer to any question I ever asked in all my years of teaching.

While the students were doing their research, I would walk around the room and look over their shoulders and ask how things were going and just, in general, check on progress.

In particular I liked to check in on the group that had chosen to research Columbia University located in New York City. This group consisted of just two girls, and though they were fair students, there was no way either of them would ever get into Columbia. Every time I would walk by them, I would ask another little checkup-type question.

"So, are you learning a lot?" I would ask.

"Yes, Mr. Crosby," they would say.

The next time around I would ask, "Do you think either of you might want to go to Columbia?"

"Oh, yes. It's a wonderful school, Mr. Crosby."

The next time, "It must be pretty expensive to go there. Have you learned how much it costs per year."

"Not yet but that's next on our research list, Mr. Crosby."

Then, about the fifth time around, I asked the magic question.

"What's the mascot of Columbia? Have you run across that yet?"

"The mascot? What do you mean mascot?"

They looked at each other—each hoping the other would know.

"You know . . . the mascot. Every school has a mascot."

I encountered nothing but blank stares.

I elaborated, "Florida State is the Seminoles. University of Florida is the Gators. U of M is the Hurricanes. What is Columbia?"

"Oh, that's what you mean by mascot."

(See. I told you neither of these girls was in danger of getting accepted to Columbia.)

"Yeah, so now that you know what a mascot is, can you tell me what Columbia's mascot is?"

I could see the wheels turning. They wanted to impress me with their knowledge of Columbia, and because this seemed like such an easy question, especially since they had been researching for a couple of days already, I guess they thought they should take a stab.

"Well . . . uh . . ." started the brighter of the two. She paused briefly to cogitate, and then using every ounce of logic stored in her body she came out with this, "Is it the . . . *taxi drivers?*"

"The taxi drivers?" I repeated unable to stifle a raucous guffaw. "Are you serious?"

It was obvious she was.

"No, it's not the taxi drivers," I howled. "What makes you think it's the taxi drivers?"

"Well, there are so many taxi cabs in New York City, I thought maybe the drivers would be a good mascot."

"Oh, I see. That's some excellent logic on your part, but I'm afraid the real mascot is the Lions. They are the Columbia Lions."

"Really? Why the Lions?"

"I don't know. Maybe you can learn that in the course of your research."

"Okay, we'll try; but, Mr. Crosby?

"Yes."

"I like the taxi drivers better."

"Me too," I said and quickly moved along to the next group.

THE NICEST PERSON IN THE UNIVERSE

Most schools have the senior class elect Senior Superlatives—you know, Most Likely to Succeed, Most Popular, Nicest Eyes, etc. Many times the suggestion was made in yearbook class, as a way to fill up a couple of pages when no other brilliant ideas were forthcoming, that we copy the Senior Superlative idea and extend it to teachers by electing Teacher Superlatives. I always thought that was a lousy idea for many reasons so I never let it get off the ground.

But on occasion I would wonder to myself, "What if we did elect teacher superlatives? Would there be any sure bets? Would there be any categories where it would be a guaranteed runaway in favor of one person?"

I came to determine that, in my mind at least, there was really only one category that would be a sure thing, a slam dunk, a take it to the bank, a bet your life savings on it. If we had a category called Nicest Person, even though we have a school full of nice people, I truly think it would be a landslide in favor of our attendance secretary Linda Castelli.

She's not just nice to a select few. She is totally nice to everyone. Everyone knows it. Everyone sees it. Everyone would vote for her. In fact, she not only is the nicest person at our school, she might just be the nicest person in the universe.

One day, about three weeks before Christmas, my wife and I were in Target looking for a small Christmas tree for my 93-year-old mother who lives in a very small apartment in an assisted-living facility. The trees we were looking at were only about a foot and a half or two feet tall at the most, but then my mother's apartment did not have room for anything any larger than that.

As we were looking at the small trees, someone came up behind us and said, "Oh, come on. Splurge. You can afford something bigger than that."

When I turned around, who should I see but none other than that ultra-nice secretary Linda Castelli.

"Hey, Linda, Merry Christmas."

"Same to you, thank you," came the reply.

"This tree isn't for us. It's for my mother, and she has a very small apartment," I felt obligated to explain.

"I was just kidding," she said.

"Oh, by the way, Linda, this is my wife Mikki. Mik, this is Linda Castelli, a secretary at school."

That's when the closest thing to a put down I've ever heard Linda Castelli utter came out of her mouth.

In an aside, kind of out of the corner of her mouth so Mikki wouldn't hear it, Linda said, "Gee, she's really pretty. What's she doing with you?"

It wasn't meant to be a put down. It was a joke. I knew it, and thought nothing of it. In fact, I played along with it. I said right back to Linda, "Yeah, well, my wife is legally blind, so she doesn't really know just how bad I look."

At first, Linda thought I was serious about the blindness.

"Oh, I'm so sorry," she said.

"She's not really blind. I was just responding to your question about why she's with me."

We laughed, but Linda's laugh seemed a little uncomfortable.

We made small talk for another minute or so and then said our good-byes. Even then I still sensed a little bit of anxiety in Linda.

The following Monday during yearbook class my student editor and I had to make a long distance call regarding some yearbook pictures. There are only a couple of phones in our school where one can make a long distance call and one of those is in Linda Castelli's office. As soon as we walked into her office, she began her apologies.

"I'm so sorry about Saturday. I was just kidding around when I said that about your wife being pretty so why is she with you. She really is pretty but . . . well, over the weekend I thought about how terrible what I said must have sounded. I felt so bad about it I almost called you to apologize. If I had had your phone number, I would have called. It was terrible of me. I still can't believe I said it."

"Are you for real?" I asked.

"Absolutely. I felt terrible. That was just an awful thing for me to say though I was just joking."

"Believe me; I didn't give it another thought. It didn't bother me in the slightest. I knew you were kidding."

That seemed to make her feel a little better though I could tell she genuinely was deeply concerned that maybe she had scarred me for life.

Anyway, my editor and I made our call. While I was on the phone, Laverne, my editor, struck up a conversation with Mrs. Castelli. When I hung up, I realized they were talking about nicknames so I couldn't resist a little joke of my own.

"You know," I said, "I have a nickname. Tell Mrs. Castelli my nickname, Laverne."

"We call him the Proof-fessor. Get it? He's our teacher and sort of like a professor, but he's always going over proofs of our pages so we call him "The Proof-fessor" instead of "The Professor."

"That's cute," said Linda with that ever-present smile of hers.

Then with as straight a face as I could muster, I said, "No, Laverne, not that nickname. That's my old nickname. Haven't you heard about my new one?"

"No, you have a new nickname?"

Linda Castelli chimed in, "Why? The Proof-fessor is such a cute nickname for you."

"Yeah, but the new one is so much more appropriate."

"More appropriate than 'The Proof-fessor'? What could be more appropriate than that?"

I paused a moment.

They were both anxious to hear my new nickname.

"Yeah, I liked being called 'The Proof-fessor' but now with the recent happening from this past weekend everyone just calls me "The ugly guy with the good-looking wife."

Laverne laughed.

Linda did not.

Even now, over a year later, she's still apologizing for something that never warranted an apology in the first place.

I told you she's the nicest person in the universe.

STRAIGHT A'S

Making straight A's has to be the ultimate goal of all serious students. Adoring parents go gaga when their kids bring home report cards showing all A's. Teachers love any student who exerts the energy and effort and puts in the necessary time that it takes to make an A in their classes. But when a kid can make an A in every single class on his schedule . . . well, that is a big, fat, hairy deal. I mean, come on, what's not to love about straight A's?

Our daughter made straight A's in college a time or two, and her mom and I were ecstatic about it. Of course, my wife Mikki gave Lindy all the credit for it, but I felt strongly that it was her father's influence during her formative years that was the single most contributing factor to her outstanding accomplishment.

Meanwhile our son Andy made straight A's too, but his . . . well, his were of a different variety. Whereas he never actually made straight A's on his report card, he did amass a string of A's in college that, though it may not actually be a record, I think you'll agree is way above average. I'm talking, of course, about . . . girlfriends. Yep, girl friends.

Now, you're probably thinking, "What kind of father is this guy? He rates his son's girlfriends?"

That is not at all what I'm talking about. I would never rate my son's girlfriends. Rather, I am talking about their names. Get this. His first girlfriend was named <u>A</u>bby. After <u>A</u>bby he moved on to <u>A</u>nna. He dated her for a while and then went back to <u>A</u>bby. Again that didn't last so he moved on once again—this time to <u>A</u>my. The <u>A</u>my thing didn't last either, and it was somewhere during the revolving door of A girls that Andy decided that maybe he needed a dog. To this day Andy is still good friends with all of the A girls who were once his girlfriends, and so he and <u>A</u>nna went to the dog pound to select a dog for Andy.

As fate would have it, they got there a few minutes before the doors opened and while they were waiting, they struck up a conversation with a lady who was there to turn in her dog. Andy immediately took a liking to the dog. He and <u>A</u>nna both thought the dog was great and quizzed the lady as to why she was getting rid of such a nice dog.

She was moving into an apartment from a house with a big yard, and there would be no place for a dog. That did it. Andy decided that was the dog for him, and he took the dog on the spot. The dog's name was . . . <u>A</u>li, and yes, the dog was female.

All this took place while Andy was in college. Now he is out and has a job teaching school. He also has another girlfriend.

When he first told us about the new girlfriend, I was a little disappointed when I learned her name. I just knew he would pick another A girl, but he told us her name was Nez.

"Oh, no, Andy, not Nez. I don't have anything against her name, but up until now you had straight A's."

"Huh?" said Andy seemingly not realizing that all of his previous girlfriends had names beginning with A.

I elaborated.

"You know, <u>A</u>bby, <u>A</u>nna, <u>A</u>bby, <u>A</u>my, and even <u>A</u>li. Their names all start with the letter A. I was bragging to my teacher friends at school that you had straight A's so to speak."

"Well, if that's all you're worried about, you can relax. Everybody calls her Nez, but her real name is <u>A</u>ryanez. In fact, it's even better than that. Her last name is . . . <u>A</u>lburquerque."

See? I told you my boy had straight A's.

LET SOMEONE ELSE DO IT! PLEASE!!!

There was a commercial a few years ago featuring a character known as Mr. Goodwrench. Not being much of a commercial watcher as a rule, I don't really remember what Mr. Goodwrench was advertising. Maybe deep down the few times I did watch I just resented the heck out of the guy because he seemed to be the direct antithesis of me. After all, my own beloved children have been known to refer to their dear old dad as "Mr. Badwrench." And though I hate to admit it, such a moniker is well deserved.

If the truth be known, I can't fix anything. I can't build anything. I can't assemble anything. No one knows this better about me than I know it about myself. And because I know it so well and because I have such a consistent record of ineptitude regarding this type of thing, I am still baffled as to how I could have let happen what happened to me one day in our school library.

It was the day's last period which also was my planning period. Like most teachers with last period planning, I think, my main concern during that free period was to make sure I had my ducks in a row for the next day. Usually this consisted of two things: a) making my lesson plans, and b) doing my Xeroxing. On this particular day it was the latter of these tasks that led to my utter consternation and embarrassment.

I had arrived at the back room of the library where the Xerox machine is located with my items to be copied in hand when I noticed the light flashing on the machine. The corresponding message read, "Replace the toner cartridge."

Well, of course, it didn't mean me—not Mr. Badwrench. It meant find the librarian, find another teacher; heck, find a kid, but no matter what, don't you, Mr. Badwrench, even think about attempting to "replace the toner cartridge."

The problem was there was no one else. It was a ghost town back there, and I needed to finish that darned copying and head for home. So with desperation as a motivator, I succumbed to the temptation to try it.

As I said, if left to my own devices, I can't ever seem to get this type of thing right, but at least with this particular thing, I had observed others doing it. I knew the doors had to be opened. I knew the cartridge had to be removed and a new one had to be inserted in its place. Then the doors had to be closed and voila; it was done. It seemed easy as pie. "Why would a college graduate with a Master's Degree not be able to do this," I asked myself.

"Because it's you, Mr. Badwrench," should have been the resounding answer. And it should have continued with, "If you go ahead with this, you know you will dumb it up somehow.

Your moniker will be expanded from Mr. Badwrench to Mr. Stupid Badwrench."

I opened the doors anyway.

There it was—the jug-like vessel known as the toner cartridge. I grasped its handle, paused for a second, and then tugged. It didn't budge. I tugged again. Nothing. Wait a minute. What's this? There was a little green lever in front of the cartridge. It looked like some sort of locking device. I pushed it from right to left and magically the cartridge was released. This time when I tugged on its handle, it came right out. Pride swelled in me. Phase one was complete and nothing was broken.

On the shelf next to the machine I saw a box containing a new cartridge. I opened it and took out the contents. It was identical to the cartridge I had just removed from the machine so I put the new one in the vacated slot and shoved. It went right in. This was going way too well. Was I actually going to be able to pull this off I wondered?

As I closed to doors to the machine, I remembered having seen our librarian remove a tab from the cartridge I had witnessed her install. I hadn't done that so I reopened the doors.

It was there all right—the little yellow tab that held all the toner in the jug. It was sticking right out there just begging to be yanked. I knew that performing that small task was all that was keeping me not only from accomplishing my goal of loading the toner but possibly even making me feel good enough about myself to at least debate the Mr. Badwrench tag the next time it was used to refer to me. Thus with a big smile on my face, I grasped the yellow tab and pulled hard.

That's when the unspeakable, the unthinkable, the unbelievable occurred. I had known all along I wouldn't be able to make this project happen successfully. What puzzled me from the outset, of course, was not *if* I would screw it up but *how* I would screw it up. Now I knew.

With the forceful pulling of the yellow tab out flew the cartridge. It zoomed from its perch in the machine and landed squarely at my feet where it promptly emptied all of its dirty black toner contents in one gigantic pile on the floor.

"Oh my God!" I yelled.

Then, in a calmer, quieter voice, I said to myself, "Nice job, Mr. Absolutely, Totally, 100% Stupid Badwrench. How did you manage this, you big boob?"

At that point the green lever caught my attention. I had neglected to return it to the locked position before yanking on the yellow tab.

That's how I had managed to screw it up, but what was I to do now to clean it up?

"Hold on a second," I thought to myself. "There's still no one here. No one has seen this catastrophe take place. I can just go back to my room, and no one will ever know I am the one who made this mess."

With a bit of a guilty conscience I decided to do just that and headed for the door. When I took one last look back at my handiwork, I froze in my tracks. Footprints. Black, toner-outlined footprints. My footprints . . . and they were following me right out the door. I was doomed. Even an amateur sleuth could follow those tracks to my door and apprehend me as the culprit.

That's when Karen Donn, our librarian, walked in.

"Hi, Bob," she said.

"Hi," I returned.

"Is everything all right?" she asked. I must have looked as if I were stealing something.

I decided to fess up. My footprints would have squealed on me anyway.

"Look," I said as I pointed to the pile of toner on the floor.

It was obvious Karen didn't know my reputation or she could have avoided asking her next question.

"What happened?"

"I tried to change the toner cartridge and forgot about the little green lever."

"It's okay. I'll call a custodian to clean it up," she said almost as if she had seen this happen before.

To follow up on that idea, I asked, "Has this ever happened to anyone else?"

Her answer stopped me in my toner-covered tracks.

"Yep, one guy . . . but he's gone."

I turned stark white.

"Gone? Are you kidding? They fired him for toner spillage?"

"No, silly. He retired."

Slowly the color returned to my face, but my embarrassment over the whole incident remains to this day.

IT'S ALL ABOUT FOCUS

I coached the school golf team for three years, and I must say I enjoyed it very much. What was not to enjoy? I only coached about three days a week because course availability was limited, and, as coach, I would play right along with the players on practice days. On match days the coach isn't allowed to coach. He simply rides in a cart from group to group to see how things are going. So, in essence, I was mostly getting paid to play golf and to ride in a cart. As I said, what was not to enjoy?

Once I gave it up, I missed it . . . sort of. Maybe that's why I looked so forward to going out once each season to take pictures of the golf team for the yearbook. It usually went like this. Before they began their match, I would first take the team shot, but after taking that picture, I would head out to strategic spots on the course to get some good action shots of the golfers as they passed by. I did this while trying to remain as inconspicuous and unobtrusive as possible.

The object, as it was explained to the players by Coach Alexander, was for them to totally ignore me if they even saw me at all on the course. They were to concentrate on the golf and leave the photography to me.

One young man was not, however, able to heed this advice. As he addressed his ball in the fairway, I looked out from behind a tree about 75 yards away and with my zoom lens attached I was about to take his picture when he looked directly at me and yelled, "CAN YOU FOCUS ME ALL RIGHT? HOW DO I LOOK?"

After he hit his shot and was walking past my location, I scolded him.

"Didn't you hear what coach said? Just pretend I'm not even out here and don't worry about your picture."

"I'm sorry," he muttered and kind of hung his head as he passed by me.

I found out later he has some kind of affliction. He is a special ed. student albeit a special ed. student who is really a good golfer.

Anyway, that was last year. Fast forward one school year to the present. Again it was picture day, and again I was at the golf course ready to shoot some photos for the yearbook.

When I arrived at the course, I spotted Kevin Alexander sitting in his golf cart waiting for the rest of his players to show up.

"How ya doin', Kevin? Ready for pictures?"

"Yeah, Bob, I think so. Everyone isn't here yet, but they should be here soon."

I sat in the cart with him, and we made small talk for a minute or so until one of his players approached him.

"Coach, can I have your belt?" the young man asked.

"No, you can't have my belt. Where's your belt?" Kevin's tone reprimanded.

It was then that I noticed that this was the same young man from the year before—the one who wanted to know if he was "in focus."

"I didn't have a chance to go home from school before coming here. That's when I usually get it. I didn't go home so I don't have it."

"Too bad," said Kevin. "Guess you'll have to do without today."

Kevin had to go up to the pro shop for a second, and he left me sitting in the cart.

Amazingly, the young man addressed me.

"Sir . . . can I have your belt?"

Still miffed I guess from what he had done the year before, I was ready to lay into him when I remembered what Kevin had told me previously about this kid's "problems." Evidently due to an unfortunate incident that had occurred during his childhood, he wasn't quite the same as the others. With that in mind, I decided to approach this as a learning experience for the boy. So half jokingly, half seriously I started.

"No, you can't have my belt. I need my belt. And, besides, if your pants fall down on about the third hole, it will teach you the value of coming to the course prepared, and then it probably won't ever happen to you again."

Before he could respond, I continued, this time with the goal of making sure he understood that we didn't need a recurrence of what had happened the previous year.

"And another thing, if you see me about to take your picture while you are playing out there, just ignore me. Last year you saw me and yelled out to me. If that happens again this year, I'm not going to take your picture at all. Understand?"

His face dropped. He obviously took it as a scolding, and I really didn't mean it that way. I just wanted to get the point across so we wouldn't have a repeat of the previous year. With that in mind I tried to make it up to him by giving him an alternative . . . an alternative that had about a one in a million chance of happening but an alternative nonetheless.

"I'll tell you what I'll do. If you make a hole-in-one today, then I'll take you aside and let you pose any way you want to, and I'll take your picture and put it in the yearbook. Is that fair?"

His response is not at all what I expected.

"Sir?"

"Yes."

"If I make a hole-in-one . . ."

"Yes."

"Can I have your belt?"

I guess he really was focused after all.

MAN, WAS I ON A ROLL!

Back in the 80's I coached some pretty good volleyball teams. Not only were my players decent athletes, but also they had a willingness to work hard to become better volleyball players. That's what made me suggest to them that we take a trip to Tallahassee one summer to participate in the FSU high school volleyball camp. I saw it as a chance to improve my team as well as an opportunity to visit my brother who just happened to live in Tallahassee.

The plan was a simple one. Since only seven players were making the trip, we would drive up in my van. They would participate in the week-long camp each day and live with about 400 other campers in the on-campus dorm which was provided by FSU. I, meanwhile, wanted no part of the dorm (other than for meals) so I would go to the practices and games with them each day and I would eat my meals with them as well. But when it was time for beddy-bye, I would spend the night at my brother's house in the comfort of an actual bed rather than on campus on a lumpy dorm bed.

After one particularly grueling day of camp, we couldn't wait to get back to the dorm for dinner. It was a cafeteria-style set up where people could go through the line and select from a number of different items. The main difference between this cafeteria and most was in the arrangement of the food. It was displayed in three sections. Along the left wall were the desserts. In the middle were the entrees. Along the right wall were the bread offerings. It was kind of a squared off horseshoe-type effect if you can imagine that.

Anyway, I had just selected my entree and was eyeballing the bread when I noticed that there was only one roll left and Theresa Hunter, one of my favorite players, was standing in front of it about to put it on her tray.

Always on the lookout for ways build team chemistry by teasing, joking with, or harassing my players, I decided this was a golden opportunity to do just that. I leapt to her side, placed my tray next to hers, and snatched the roll before she could take it.

"DON'T TOUCH THAT ROLL!" I practically screamed at her.

She was obviously surprised by my little stunt as she nearly jumped out of her shoes.

I laughed like crazy as I placed the roll on my tray and turned to see how she had enjoyed my little shenanigan.

I remember being shocked to discover that she was not laughing or even slightly amused by my maneuver. But as shocked as I was that she wasn't laughing, I was even more shocked by the fact that *she wasn't Theresa Hunter*! In fact, she wasn't anyone I had ever even seen before much less knew.

"Ohmigosh," I stammered. "I'm so sorry. I thought you were one of my players. Here, I didn't mean to steal your roll. Please take it. I was just playing a trick on my player, but it turns out you aren't my player. From behind you look just like her, but in actuality it seems you aren't her at all." A more ridiculous stream of rambling tripe I had never uttered in my entire life.

Her reply was much more concise than my babbling folderol.

"I don't want it now," was her highly indignant retort as she turned and stomped off in complete disgust.

Boy, did I feel dumb. At least none of my players had seen it happen. They would have never let me live it down.

Whereas I don't think I had ever seen the girl whose roll I snatched before the incident occurred, after it happened, I seemed to see her everywhere. And each time our paths crossed she looked even more miffed at me than she did the time before.

I guess some people just can't take a joke.

<u>ODDS AND ENDS</u>

There have been many brief incidents that come to mind that are not quite long enough for chapters unto themselves so I have decided to put a few of them together in this chapter of "odds and ends."

And speaking of odd, one of our assistant principals tells the story of a young man who was continually getting into trouble. Because his mother was a cafeteria worker at our school, the AP tried on several occasions to cut the young man some slack in his punishment. Eventually, however, he stepped way over the line, and the AP had no choice but to suspend him.

Of course, the mother came to the AP's office to plead on her son's behalf.

"Why are you suspending my son?"

"I had no choice. Had any other student done what he did, they would have gotten the same punishment. I can't give your son a break on this one."

"But you aren't taking into account his condition," came the defense from the mother.

"Oh yeah? What condition is that?" the AP wanted to know.

"He's ODD," offered the mother.

"Man is he ever! But being "odd" is no excuse for breaking the rules" the AP couldn't help but think but was too nice to say.

Instead, she asked, "You mean ADD don't you? According to the teachers, it seems that about half our students have ADD (Attention Deficit Disorder)."

"Oh, he has ADD too," countered the mom, "but it's the ODD that gets him in trouble."

"Oh really? How in the world can being odd have anything to do with his breaking the rules?"

Then came the surprising reply.

"Because his having Oppositional Defiant Disorder (ODD) is what causes him to act up."

"Oh, that ODD," came the brief reply.

The punishment, however, remained the same, ODD notwithstanding.

· · ·

Maybe one of the oddest things I ever saw at school happened one day as I was taking my class to the library.

It was first period of the day, and after the morning announcements and taking roll, I explained our purpose in going to the library. I also gave an additional admonishment.

"Just walk straight to the library. Don't dawdle along the way, and don't look through the windows in the doors of the other classrooms to wave to your friends. There's nothing going on in those rooms worth looking at anyway," I said.

Between my room and the library, there are four class-rooms on one side of the hall and two on the other side. Unlike the kids, I never stop to wave to students or teachers in those classrooms, but like the kids, I can't seem to resist looking in as I pass by.

On this particular day I saw something that I had never seen before. As I passed by my friend Chris Donahue's room, I saw her students all looking intently up toward the top of the chalkboard in the corner of the room.

But that wasn't what was odd. No, the odd part was see-ing Chris with a manila folder in her hands and her hands held high above her head as she continuously jumped up and down. She was facing away from the students and toward the chalkboard. And even odder was the fact that not one of her students was laughing. They were all staring intently at something that seemed to be on the chalkboard.

"What the heck is that all about?" I wondered, but with my students already on their way to the library, I didn't have time to stop and ask or even to watch a little longer to try to figure it out myself.

At lunch I saw Chris.

"What in the world were you doing this morning—your morning calisthenics?" I asked her.

"When?"

"I took my class to the library first period, and as I passed by your room I saw you holding a manila folder over your head and jumping up and down."

"Oh, that. We were watching television."

"Huh?"

"The television set in my room is on a high shelf behind the pull down board in the corner of the room. So everyone was watching the TV. I was showing *The Crucible*. You know that first scene where all the girls go into the woods and are dancing around?"

"Yeah."

"Well, several of those girls are naked, and we aren't allowed to show nudity in school. But that is such a good movie and helps them to visualize the play so much better that I couldn't resist showing it. I didn't want to get in trouble though so I was using the manila folder to block the view of the naked girls from my students' sight."

Right then I knew why Chris is such a good teacher. She is soooooooooooooooooooooooooooo creative.

. . .

To avoid going stark raving loony teachers occasionally have to have some sort of diversion. What better way to do that than a good old pool? Not a swimming pool. Nope. A good old friendly, innocent, everybody under the sun including doctors, lawyers, judges, etc., does it so why not teachers, betting pool. And what better place to put this story than a brief chapter on odds (and ends)?

For about the past 12 years or so I have sponsored/supervised four pools a year. At the beginning of the year, there was the NFL Bridge Pool. Each participant puts in $10.00 one time and picks one NFL game a week, not against the spread just the outright winner. As long as he picks a winner he is still in. If his team loses, he's done. A team can only be picked once, however, just to make it a little more difficult. (We named it the NFL Bridge Pool because if a person's team loses, he is out of the pool, and he feels like jumping off a bridge.)

Then there was the college bowl pool, the Super Bowl squares, and the NCAA March Madness pool. I kept track of the money and the stats for each pool. I paid the winners and commiserated with the losers one of whom was usually me.

Anyway, one day during yearbook class, the students were busy at the computers when a teacher friend of mine walked in to turn in his college bowl picks. Paper clipped to his three sheets was a five and four one-dollar bills (three dollars per sheet was the entry fee).

"Hey, Kenny, got the winning sheets there?"

"No, I never win, but it's fun playing anyway. So, here's my nine-dollar donation."

"Great, I'll put you in the computer. Good luck."

As Kenny left, I was shocked to see that one of my students had witnessed the entire scene brief though it was.

This was no dumb girl, and she thought she had it figured out.

"Mr. Crosby, can I ask you a question?"

"You just did," I replied as I always did whenever anyone prefaced a question in that way.

"No, I mean another question."

"Sure, go ahead."

"I've seen you take sheets of paper and money from not just that teacher but other teachers too and I was wondering . . ."

"Yes, what were you wondering?"

"Are you a bookie?"

My response was succinct and honest. It was truly how I viewed myself with regard to our pools and what they provided for my fellow teachers and me.

"No, my dear," I said. "I'm . . . the recreation director!"

"Oh," she said. "You must do a good job. People seem awfully happy to hand you their money."

"That's exactly the purpose of the recreation director . . . to make people happy," I said with a smile.

Always happy to educate today's youth, I was proud that I was able to teach at least one student the difference between a bookie and a recreation director.

SOMETIMES WE JUST LOSE IT . . . COMPLETELY*

When I first started teaching back in the 70's, I was also an assistant football coach. The head coach was a stickler for discipline. He insisted on promptness to practice, wearing ties on game days, and no cussing.

He even set a good example in the no cussing area by never cussing himself. Oh, he wanted to . . . often . . . but he never did. In fact, when he was really upset with a player, he would scream the player's last name at the top of his lungs but only after he had first yelled his version of a swear word. That swear word? Crimanutley. It is pronounced "cry•muh•nutley" and it could be heard several times every day at practice.

The usage I heard the most was directed at James Wolf, our lanky tight end who would screw up on a fairly regular daily basis. "CRIMANUTLEY, WOLF, can't you get anything right?" Coach Armstrong would yell.

Other names like Ruffin, Thomas, and Smith were fairly frequently heard too.

"CRIMANUTLEY, Ruffin, quit jumpin' offsides."

"CRIMANUTLEY, Thomas, hang on to the doggone ball."

"CRIMANUTLEY, Smith, can't you ever remember the snap count?"

I heard each of these so often they are indelibly ingrained in my brain. But the one I wanted to hear, the one I absolutely longed to hear, I only heard once in my two years there. You see our best player was a little running back by the name of Terry Hutley. He was a good kid and an even better player. He seldom made a mistake, but secretly I always wished he would. Every day I would go to practice and hope that Terry Hutley would screw up. I thirsted for it.

One day at practice it happened. A running play was called—a pitchout to Hutley going around the left end. But when the ball was snapped and everybody went left, Hutley didn't. He went right. It was obviously his mistake. Everybody knew it.

Out it came.

"CRIMANUTLEY, Hutley, run the right play!"

Even back then I had a fondness for silly rhymes, and I lost control. I could see it coming, but I still couldn't contain myself. As I laughed, the players laughed right along with me. Hearing their always serious coach yell "Crimanutley, Hutley" at the top of his lungs was comical to them too.

It wasn't quite as comical when they ran an extra 30 minutes of gassers after practice. Nor was it funny when coach laid into me while they were running.

I acted as contrite as I could, but really, with my affinity for rhymes, it took all I could do to keep from losing it again.

When I got in the car to go home, I remember scolding myself, "CRIMANUTLEY, Crosby" . . . and then I began to laugh some more.

. . .

At the complete opposite end of the spectrum from "Crimanutley, Hutley," is this incident. A good teacher friend of mine told me this, and it is with his permission that I reprint it here. Though I never got this carried away, I know exactly how my friend felt. In fact, all teachers know. I doubt that there's a teacher anywhere who hasn't been this exasperated, but I also doubt that many of us would have the guts to handle a similar situation the way my friend did. Here's the way it went.

There was a girl in his Algebra II Honors class who wasn't cutting the mustard. She was very apathetic regarding the work and also had a very negative attitude about life in general. The rest of the class was outstanding. They were bright and eager to learn.

One day the girl came to class, plopped her books down on the desk, and began what seemed to be her own private tirade against the world. In the space of about a minute my teacher buddy heard the word "shit" used by this young lady at least five different times. She wasn't talking to anyone in particular; in fact, she was basically muttering under her breath the whole time, but the main word that seemed to be distinguishable was "shit." My friend had had enough. He wanted to put a stop to it while at the same time he wanted to show her just how ridiculous she sounded. Thus, he launched into a tirade of his own.

"LOOK, I'VE ABOUT HAD IT WITH YOUR SHIT, LITTLE MISS SHIT FOR BRAINS. YOU HAVEN'T BEEN HERE

TWO MINUTES, AND I'VE HEARD YOU USE THE WORD SHIT FIVE TIMES ALREADY. IT'S BULLSHIT, AND IT'S BULLSHIT THAT IS GOING TO STOP. IN FACT, IF YOU DON'T PUT AN END TO THIS SHIT, I'LL PERSONALLY STOP THE SHIT MYSELF BY WRITING YOU A REFERRAL, AND THAT'S WHEN THE SHIT WILL REALLY HIT THE FAN. YOU MAY NOT GIVE A SHIT, BUT I DO, AND BE-CAUSE I DO, YOU ARE ABOUT TO BE UP SHIT'S CREEK. SO WHAT IF YOU'VE HAD A SHITTY DAY SO FAR, THAT'S TOUGH SHIT, AND I DON'T GIVE A SHIT IF YOU HAVE. BUT UNDERSTAND THIS—YOU DON'T KNOW JACK SHIT, YOU LITTLE SHIT, IF YOU THINK YOU CAN COME INTO MY ROOM AND USE THE WORD SHIT OVER AND OVER AND THINK I'M GOING TO IGNORE THAT SHIT. THAT'S SOME MAJOR BULLSHIT, OR MAYBE IT'S SOME MAJOR HORSESHIT, BUT EITHER WAY IT'S SOME SHIT THAT'S GOING TO STOP. AND IF YOU THINK I'M KID-DING, YOU DON'T KNOW SHIT FROM SHINOLA."*

By the time he was finished, the rest of the class had lapsed into complete shock. My friend was red in the face, and the object of his wrath could only stare at him slack-jawed.

One thing was for sure though. He never heard her use the word "shit" again.

*Yes, the "shit" story, just like all the other stories in this book, is true. My friend's diatribe was similar to the wording above with the possibility of a couple of exceptions. He doesn't remember the exact wording, but he does know he used the word "shit" in as many different ways as he could on the spur of the moment.

Additionally, I would like to point out that I had intended to write this entire book without any foul language or any stories that are negative in nature. This one, however, is the exception, and that is why I have saved it for last. Besides, it is very sad but true that it is virtually impossible to walk down a crowded corridor in a public high school anymore without hearing all sorts of profanity. F-bombs and other profanity galore seem to be prominent themes nowadays. Thus, I really did want to include the "shit" story in the book as it was one teacher's odd but effective attempt to combat the profanity issue. His harangue has become legendary at our school and deserves its rightful place among the other stories.

POSTSCRIPT

Got a funny story from your school days? It doesn't have to be "hold your sides while you laugh out loud" funny. It only needs to be a little amusing, entertaining, or interesting. It does, however, have to have happened in school.

The stories you have read in *It Happened in School* are all examples of the types of stories I want. Everyone who shares the school experience has seen classes, days, events, or people in school that are just as funny or even funnier than those highlighted here. Or if not funny, then maybe they are just enjoyable stories that need to be shared. If you have a story of that nature that you would like to contribute, please email it to me at ithappenedinschool@gmail.com. Or if you just want to share your comments about *It Happened in School*, you may do that there as well.

For those who wish to share stories, you may write the story yourself or just send me the details, and I will flesh it out for you. Either way, it may appear in book two of *It Happened in School* whereupon you will be properly acknowledged. Anyone is welcome to submit a story, but, teachers, come on. Surely you have seen some things in your careers that will put smiles on people's faces or warm their hearts. Some of the stories you read in this book must have reminded you of similar instances that you remember fondly. If they did, then here's your chance to share those pleasant memories with the world. (No real names of students, please!!)

Any and all stories will be considered, but I do reserve the right to edit and adjust slightly, and I further reserve the right to publish, but not guarantee to publish, any story sent to me.

ABOUT THE AUTHOR

Bob Crosby taught English for over 35 years in the public school systems of Florida. He also coached a collective total of 38 seasons of athletics including volleyball, softball, baseball, football, and golf. As journalism adviser to 27 school yearbooks and 24 school newspapers, he was recognized by the *Fort Lauderdale Sun-Sentinel* as Broward County's Journalism Adviser of the Year in 2007. Bob is retired and resides in Fort Lauderdale with his wife Mikki.